2-

THE
TWINS
A Journey of a Lifetime

Twin brothers' journey through Chicago Sports
History and their recollections of a bygone era

TONY & CARL
RUZICKA

FOREWORD BY
CHICAGO SPORTS MEDIA PERSONALITY
BRUCE LEVINE

FOREWORD

BY BRUCE LEVINE, CHICAGO
SPORTS MEDIA PERSONALITY

L IVING THE GOOD LIFE IN the brave new world of America in the 1950s, gave hope to a wide spectrum of possibilities for the young post-World War II men and women of the "Great Generation". These hard-nosed people, you must understand, had dreams to fulfill, with children to raise, that would be unthinkable in the decades to come. Television, space travel, counter-culture revolutions, and the computer world would all be ahead in the next years and century.

Like the authors' parents, Anthony and Martha Ruzicka, my mother and father grew up in the great depression years preceding and following the Stock Market Crash of 1929. With jobs in short supply and times difficult at best, these very special kids and young adults rolled up their sleeves and worked hard at any menial job they could find while learning trades and seeking education with the promise of a better life. This was the American dream that immigrant parents sought while leaving the "old country" in the late 19th and early 20th centuries. With World War II now in the rearview mirror, this new rising society had the belief that any career and future dreams would be easy to accomplish after having survived their previous 20 years of life and death struggles on a daily basis. However, those dreams would mostly wait to be fulfilled by their newborn sons and daughters of the baby boomer era.

Tony and Carl Ruzicka were the recipients of the middle-class upbringing in the blue-collar mecca of a city named Cicero, an area just west of Chicago's downtown. In the 1920s, mobster Al Capone headed up his gang in this large city. The heart and soul of Cicero was the hardcore worker and church-going resident laboring toward the American dream of a home and a good-paying job to provide for his/her family.

Twin brothers born one minute apart on May 22, 1949, the third and fourth children of the Ruzicka clan, Tony and Carl would start the next chapter of America's history with their "new generation". It must be noted that on the day the twins were born, in typical Chicago Cubs fashion, the north siders lost a game to the Boston Braves by a score of 7 to 2. The Cubs starting pitcher, with the longest name in baseball history, Calvin Coolidge Julia Ceaser Tuskahoma McLish, would hit a home run during the loss in front of 15,113 Wrigley Field partisans. This once proud franchise, winners of a league-high 10 pennants between 1906 and 1945, would finish in the second division of the National League every season from 1947 to 1966. The Ruzicka twins were destined to cheer for this downtrodden group of players and characters who made up the Chicago National League club without much distinction for most of their youth. Time spent playing ball in the street and schoolyards of Chicagoland in the 1950s was safe haven and great fun. Loyalty, friendship, and charity were values taught by Tony and Carl's folks. Thus, cheering for the local rag/tag group of baseball players was not difficult when you had faith that the next day, or in the Cubs' case, the next decade could be a better one.

In this book, you will meet sports legends George Halas, Ernie Banks, Yosh Kawano, Mike Ditka, Bill Bishop, Pierre Pilote, and Chico Maki. You will find out that the most unlikely people to have friendships with the "rich and famous" may, indeed, be living in the bungalows of the neighborhood you live in now, or once did in the past. These "rich and famous" athletes may be living in similar bungalows. You will learn of their pure joy of buying and trading Topps baseball cards and of their receiving Hartland figurines of Ernie Banks, Babe Ruth, and Nellie Fox in perfect miniature molds of their likeness; of their magical experience of running home from school and seeing Frank Ernaga and Cuno Barrigan hit home runs for the Cubs in their first at-bats; of their seeing umpire Vic Delmore allow two balls in play at the same time in the wackiest moment in baseball history; and of their being on the field for the 1963 NFL Championship game between the Chicago Bears (14-10 winners) and the New York Giants. This experience would make the 14 year-old Ruzicka twins the most famous Cicero residents this side of former Bears tackle Bill Bishop.

The story that these two friends of mine have to offer is about living each day with a purpose; that hard work, while smiling and laughing at whatever fate would bring their way, will prevail. Both of these fine gentlemen have lived that good life from the perspective of being rich in character and being men of honor. They will show you, in this enjoyable walk through the decades, how having goals and values, while living up to those golden rules, is the true reward for a life well-lived.

Join these proud Cicero natives in reliving the coming age for America and Chicagoans. They present a fascinating life and reveal real people who became their friends and helped shape the journey they have taken for 71 years.

Find out how being aggressive and not taking "no" as an answer, led them on a magic carpet ride of historic moments with giants in the sports world. How many 13 year-olds can say NFL founder George Halas would become a focal point for their hard work and success? The Ruzicka twins can tell you they were hired by Papa Bear himself.

Tony and Carl will take you in a time machine back to when neighborhoods and neighbors were essential to learning life. Growing up in a small section of a giant metropolis like Cicero, Illinois, these two fun-loving brothers take you on "L" rides, car trips, and walks through decades of their love of Chicago sports and the people who made history around the games.

Enjoy this wonderful life journey by two of my favorite people. They will entertain you with a tour of Chicago while growing up in simpler times, during this very special post-war time of the "50s and 60s". You will marvel at how easily they made high profile friends, while becoming successful businessmen and raising families along the way. As the anarchist Abby Hoffman one titled his autobiography, if you can't afford it, "steal this book"!

Tony and Carl offered remuneration for this foreword. Having known them both for over 45 years, their friendship and kindness have more than paid forward this brief look into their last six decades of sport and social consciousness in Chicago, the greatest city ever created. Enjoy the indomitable Ruzicka twins' zest for life, liberty, and the pursuit of sport happiness, despite the Cubs college of coaches and the 1-13 Bears 1969 season.

Bruce Levine
May 2020

INTRODUCTION

HELLO! WE ARE TWIN BROTHERS, Tony and Carl Ruzicka. Growing up in the late 1950s and early 1960s in Cicero, Illinois, a suburb just west of Chicago, we were sports fans. Life seemed much simpler back then. Sports, while important, did not serve as the huge, money-making industry it is today. Each town seemed like a true community. Each neighborhood had its own school. Students, "gifted" or not, living within the school's boundaries, had to attend that school. Each neighborhood had its own bank and savings & loan. Mortgages were made by and stayed with the local institution. For the most part, families could happily sustain themselves with one income-earning parent. The Prudential Building at 601 vertical feet was Chicago's tallest skyscraper. Professional athletes usually had secondary jobs in their off-season and seemed more attached to their fans.

Using our uniqueness of being twins, some courage, and our knowledge of Chicago sports, we managed to become lifelong friends with many of our heroes. These friendships, and what would appear to be pure chance, took us on a serendipitous life-time journey that would have been impossible to predict or even comprehend.

One day, at age eleven, while reading the sports page of the local newspaper, the *Cicero Life*, we were about to embark on that adventurous journey that continues to shape our lives even today at age seventy-one. Who knew that our journey would include writing this book? Hopefully, it will be a nostalgic look back at Chicago sports but also serve as an inspiration to youngsters that many things are possible if an effort is made, and to professional athletes and to all adults that their interest in youth can truly make a positive impact.

This is our story.

BACKGROUND

The Twins with Spotty

WE WERE THE YOUNGEST OF four children. Our sister Barbara was born June 21, 1940. Our older brother Tom was born on April 16, 1944. We were born on May 22, 1949. It was a Cesarean birth with Tony arriving at 2:21 a.m., then Carl at 2:22. Our mother had previously had one ovary removed as well as one-half of her remaining ovary. Her doctor told our parents they would not need to use protection when having intimate relations as she could not become pregnant. To quote Steve Stone, Chicago Cubs and Chicago White Sox announcer, when highlighting a play that could be used as a learning tool for kids first learning baseball, "Let that be a lesson to all you youngsters out there!"

On the way to the hospital, our dad said that Yale University's "Whiffenpoof Song" was being played on the radio. This would be given meaning as we got older.

Our father, Anthony James Ruzicka, Sr. (Tony's namesake), was born June 12, 1913, on the kitchen table of the family residence at 5511 West Twenty-Second Place in Cicero. He was the youngest of four children, having two older brothers, Bill and Stanley, and a sister, Lillian. She was the oldest sibling being fourteen years older than our father. Our father's parents had emigrated to the United States from what is now the Czech Republic around 1900. His mother died when he was nine months old, while his father, who had remarried, died when our father was nine years of age. Our father was raised by his stepmother, after first being passed from one aunt to another. His stepmother eventually bought the empty lot next door, built a bungalow with a garden apartment, sold 5511, and moved into the new house at 5509. True to her Bohemian heritage, the family resided in the garden apartment, saving the main quarters as an income-producing rental property.

Our father was a union printer who worked on a monotype keyboard at Hayes Lochner, Inc. Typographers, a print shop specializing in printing for advertising. Its offices were at 160 E. Illinois Street just across the street from the Chicago Tribune building and just across Michigan Avenue from the Wrigley Building. A prideful man, our father wore a suit to work each day even though he was a tradesman.

Once we turned sixteen, we worked alongside him in the summers of our last two years of high school and our four years of undergraduate school. We worked part-time at the print shop when going to graduate school.

Our mother, Martha (nee Katusic), was seven years younger than our father. She was born on August 27, 1920, in Cicero around Sixteenth Street and Fifty-Fifth Avenue. Her parents emigrated to the United States around 1910 from what is now

Croatia. She was the second youngest of five children, with an older brother, Nick, two older sisters, Emily and Helen, and one younger brother, Tom.

Our mom was primarily a housewife, charged with the responsibility of taking care of us four children. She attended all school functions and was largely in charge of discipline.

We were rarely very shy, except for dealing with girls or when dealing with facial blemishes as adolescents. We are sure that our boldness is a trait that came from our mom. In the second grade, the mothers were invited to class to sing Christmas carols. Most mothers faintly mumbled the words. Not our mom. Singing loudly and clearly, we never have heard "Silent Night" sung so beautifully! For a fundraiser for our local Boys Club, she dressed as one of the Mouseketeers on the *Mickey Mouse Club* television show.

Both of our parents were hard workers, but they knew how to have fun! Money did not seem to impress them. All of us children noticed their charity and how they felt rewarded and enriched by their friendships. They had a gift for seeing others' points of view.

Martha & Tony Ruzicka
(Parents) wedding

Martha & Tony
Ruzicka (Parents)

3

Cicero was a thriving blue-collar suburb located just west of Chicago. Our home was approximately seven miles west and three miles south of the heart of downtown. Cicero residents were primarily of Czech and Italian heritage, and its population was about 60,000 people. Western Electric Company, which made parts for then Bell Telephone (later becoming AT&T) was the main source of employment. We lived one block south of Twenty-second Street, which was renamed Cermak Road after Anton Cermak, the Chicago mayor who died of a gunshot that was intended for President Franklin Roosevelt. A mile-long stretch along Cermak Road was the home of First National Bank of Cicero, Western National Bank, Clyde Federal Savings & Loan, and Mid America Savings & Loan. It is said that this stretch had more cumulative wealth than Wall Street. Cicero was also known for its two racetracks, Sportsman's Park and Hawthorne.

However, its single most noted claim to fame was that it was the headquarters for Al Capone. The Al Capone era was made famous through the weekly television series, *The Untouchables,* starring Robert Stack as Elliott Ness. Al Capone's brother, Ralph, resided in Cicero as did other later Chicago mob fixtures. As children, we were excited to hear references to Cicero while watching the television series, especially when they made references to Capone's henchmen, the Genna Brothers. Their great-nephews were our classmates. Because our father wore a fedora, he was often mistaken for one of the Capones. We took pride in the fact that Frank Nitti committed suicide along the railroad tracks roughly two miles from our house.

It was said that one of our maternal grandmother's jobs was doing the laundry and other housekeeping chores for Tony Accardo, boss of the Chicago Outfit at his River Forest home. For a short time, our brother Tom dated Paula Glimco, a relation of Joey Glimco, Chicago's top labor racketeer. He would take her dancing on the *Chicago Bandstand* television show. The show was broadcast live from the Chicago Merchandise Mart, from four to five o'clock. We would rush home from school to watch him dance on Channel 5, Chicago's NBC affiliate. After a few dates, Tom wanted to date someone else but was afraid to tell Paula and face possible repercussions from the Mob.

Unfortunately, Cicero was also known for being a segregated town. A few blacks were "allowed" to work there, but never, ever live there. Cash, the soda and luncheon attendant at Pavlicek's Drug Store, and Tony, the mailman, stand out as men of color whom we were privileged to know. We thought nothing of our mom inviting Tony into the house to share a cup of coffee.

Our love for sports was influenced primarily by our brother Tom. He, in turn, was influenced by our father's brother, our Uncle Bill, and by our mom's brothers, our Uncle Nick, and our Uncle Tom. All were fans, especially of the Chicago Cubs. Uncle Nick and Uncle Tom played football and baseball. They followed the Cicero Boosters, who believe it or not, once played against the Chicago Bears. They told the story of as kids asking Bronko Nagurski if they could tackle him. Bronko complied and momentarily hurt his shoulder.

Our dad and mom showed little interest in sports, save for the fact that they supported our interests. However, every year our dad would take us to Chicago Stadium to watch the Golden Gloves boxing tournament. Three rings were filled with continuous action. One boxer we saw was Cassius Clay, who, of course, changed his name to Muhammed Ali upon converting to Islam. Shortly after he changed his name, Carl saw him downtown while running errands for the print shop. "Great to meet you, Cassius," Carl stammered. "It's Muhammed, son," he replied.

Our dad would also take us to the stadium to see the Harlem Globetrotters. This was a real treat. Afterward, we would wait to get autographs from Meadowlark Lemon, Tex Harrison, and other members of the team.

Our brother Tom would bring home Chicago Cubs Yearbooks. We excitedly read the biographies of each player and memorized their statistics. The excitement grew as we were able to see them play on WGN television, good old Channel 9! During the summer, we watched parts of many games, although our mom implored us to play outside. During the school year, we raced home so we could watch the final few innings.

The game was followed by the "10th Inning" where Jack Brickhouse, famed Cubs announcer and recipient of the 1983 Ford C. Frick Award from the Baseball Hall of Fame, would "go over the unhappy totals" (the Cubs lost way more games than they won during this period) and interview one of the current players.

Our brother Tom took us to our first Cubs game in either 1955 or 1956. We vaguely remember seeing Jackie Robinson play.

It is about this time that our brother freaked us out by saying, "Tony, you are really Carl; and Carl, you are really Tony!" We shockingly resented having our characters impugned by our own brother!

We were somewhat interchangeable. Tony and Carl. Carl and Tony. It did not seem to matter.

Having been ordered by our mom to "go play outside," we joined up with our friends on the block who were all of similar age: Alan Bernard, Alan Prochaska, and Wayne Hrabak were approximately the age of older brother Tom. Dale Bernard, Larry Prochaska, and Terry Hrabak were roughly our age. We were joined later by a newcomer on the block, Bill Coulson. This was an idyllic time. We always had enough boys to choose teams and play ball. The Bernards and Prochaskas were Chicago White Sox fans. The Ruzicka boys were Cubs fans. The Hrabak boys split their allegiance: Wayne cheered for the Sox, Terry for the Cubs! The division in loyalties led to many heated arguments: who was a better shortstop Ernie Banks or Luis Aparicio, the National League is superior to the American League, it is easy to hit a home run at Wrigley, etc.

As young kids, we collected baseball cards feverishly. The cards, then Topps baseball cards, came out around Easter of every spring. We all looked forward to this moment. We took great pride in the fact that our mom was the first to spot the cards while shopping and brought a few packs home for us. Each of us kept or own pack tied securely by a rubber band. For hours we would sit on each other's front steps trading cards. We would exchange cards and start the process of going through our friend's deck: "got 'em," "don't want 'em," etc. Those cards that we were interested in acquiring by trade would be put aside for negotiation. Carl remembers one special trade with Larry: Mickey Mantle to Larry for Willy Mays and Ted Kluzewski. Duplicates were fastened to the spokes of our bicycles with a clothespin. The spinning wheels resulted in the sound of a motorbike.

We have a coffee-table-sized book entitled *Topps Baseball Cards: The Complete Picture Collection, A 35 Year History, 1951-1985*. As we leaf through its pages, many cards pictured come to life with memories of us trading them on the front steps. We can almost smell the sheet of bubble gum that came with each package. What wonderful times!

We imagine we collected cards from around 1956 through around 1961 or so. We wish we never outgrew the excitement. We gave away our collection, along with our football and Davy Crockett cards, to sons of a friend of our father. We regret doing so as the cards have since become valuable. Yet, the book reminds us of a lesson we try to carry within us. The value in the cards was not their monetary value, but the memories of collecting them.

In the summer of 1958, Terry was the envy of us Cubs fans. Ernie Banks was in his newly opened pack! Ernie was our first sports hero, and gave one of our first lessons to look past one's color while living in segregated Cicero!

One day shortly after acquiring Ernie's card, Terry rang our doorbell crying hysterically. Someone had stolen it! He was inconsolable. Later that same day, Terry came over again. He was now extremely happy. His mom told him to write a letter to Ernie Banks explaining that his card had been stolen. We downplayed the whole, stupid idea! Yet, in a few weeks, Terry had once again become the envy of our block. He was the recipient of an autographed picture postcard from Ernie! This was a coup! Recognizing it as such, we immediately went home and wrote our own letters to Ernie: "Dear Ernie, I too lost your baseball card!" The returned autographed picture postcards remain in our collection. Logically, we expanded our requests to other stars like Stan Musial, star of the St. Louis Cardinals.

Terry's mom, Adeline, was a great Cubs fan. One day in the summer of 1958, while we played ball in the street, she called us in to watch Stan Musial get his 3000th hit against Moe Drabowsky of the Cubs. She was as excited and perplexed as us boys when two balls were put in play at the same time during a 1959 game at Wrigley between the Cubs and the Cardinals. Poor Ernie Banks did not know which ball to catch. What was it with those Cardinals? Every bad moment seemed to include that team!

Unfortunately, she died from cancer shortly after that. Immediately after the ambulance took her body away from their home, Terry and Wayne came to our home. Our mother gave them comfort, and we played games to divert their minds from the sadness and emptiness they felt.

Our mom, although not much interested, took us kids to Wrigley Field a few days each season. Certain days were designated as "Ladies Day" at the ballpark, and she and other supportive mothers received free admission. To our mom's dismay, all of us boys wanted to stay after the game to get autographs. We would wait in the concourse for the players to come out of the clubhouse.

We remember one day when Ernie Banks came out. We, along with a throng of other kids, surged toward Ernie for his treasured signature. Ernie proceeded to get into his car (parked in the concourse in those days), started rolling up the car window, and driving slowly away without acknowledging us adoring fans. Our mom had enough of such nonsense. Grabbing all of our scorecards, she stuck her arm in the not-completely-rolled-up window and admonished Ernie: "If you think I enjoy being at this game and then waiting for hours so the boys can get your autograph, you have a second guess coming . . . now sign these cards!"

Shamefully, Ernie complied. Ernie grew into the most beloved Cubs of all. He was one of the most fan-friendly superstars at that time. We like to think he owed it all to our mom.

We often played games in the street. Running bases, practicing fielding of grounders and flyballs, seeing who could catch the last high pop-up as nightfall was setting in. There were only a few cars parked on the street, so our games were seldom interfered with. Most of the fathers were at work or had their cars parked in the garage. The cars that remained belonged to men working various night shifts.

At a few places on the street were cutouts of the curbs which led to the sewer system. Countless times we tried to catch up to an errant ball before it rolled into the cutout and then to the sewer. Most times, we were unsuccessful. Periodically in the early fall, the town maintenance department came to clean out the sewers. We waited anxiously to see what baseballs were retrieved by the workers. Most of them were dried out and of little use, but every now and then, we were lucky. Some balls had new life!

Years later, when Tony was a trustee of the Village of Glencoe, there was a discussion about widening a road with federal dollars. A potential drawback was that the widening would interfere with the village's current sewer system. Tony suggested that they use the curb cutout system used in Cicero. He started laughing uncontrollably for no apparent reason. When questioned why he was laughing, Tony stated that although he and his brother graduated from Yale, Dale from Northern Illinois University, Larry from Ohio State University, and Wayne from DePaul, none of them ever thought of merely covering the curb cut out with a piece of cardboard.

Upon reflection, this supports the notion of "never overlook the obvious."

The phrase was to have great benefits for the Village of Glencoe when Tony became president of the village in 2001. Since his arrival in Glencoe in 1975, the "Welcome to Glencoe" sign on Green Bay Road was north of the Hubbard Woods Plaza. As a trustee, he advocated for moving the sign to the south side of the plaza just north of Scott Avenue, as property north of Scott at Green Bay was incorporated Glencoe property. As president, he convinced the U.S. Post Office to change the zip code of Hubbard Woods Plaza from 60093 (Winnetka) to 60022 (Glencoe). As a result, all the sales tax generated by Hubbard Woods Plaza business, primarily Walgreens, Binny's, Dunkin Donuts, Subway, and 7-Eleven (until a few years ago) that had previously gone to Winnetka, now goes to Glencoe. Additionally, the assessed valuation of the plaza is now part of Glencoe's real estate tax base.

"Don't overlook the obvious" later had a major impact on outpatients receiving medication from the Cook County Hospital in Chicago. When Tony was president of Glencoe, incoming Cook County Commissioner Larry Suffredin added Tony to his transition team. Tony was tasked with studying the Cook County health system. He learned that outpatients waited up to ten days for their prescriptions to be filled. The prescriptions were filled in eight county facilities, most of which were not in anyone's neighborhood. Tony suggested that Walgreens could fill the prescriptions. He met with Walgreens personnel, and eventually, his suggestion bore fruit. Outpatients could now get their prescriptions filled at their neighborhood Walgreens while doing their shopping.

In our alley, we played games of softball. Hitting into a yard was an automatic out. It definitely required us to hit "up the middle" and not pull the ball. Our sister Barbara was especially talented. Unfortunately, this skill has increasingly become a lost art in today's baseball. Hitting into a mean neighbor's yard was an automatic two outs. Hitting into the meanest neighbor's yard was an automatic three outs.

The Twins with Tom and Barbara

This was also the case when playing whiffle ball in the "mud palladium", the backyard of Dale Bernard, which did not have one blade of grass and had bricks pounded into the dirt for bases. We played with a ping pong paddle and a practice golf ball secured by tape. Other rules in this game included a balk or "gutter ball" or hitting a homer over the "pennant porch", something we incorporated from Charles Finley and his Kansas City, then Oakland, A's.

For serious nine-inning games, we all went to Sherlock School, about a block east of us. They had two cement playgrounds on either side of the school. Our favorite was the north side of the school. We played slow pitch with a regulation-sized rubber ball and "pitcher's hand out". The balls cost about twenty-five cents each. Today you can buy a dozen for about twenty-five dollars. For right-handed hitters, a ball hit to the right side of second base was an automatic out. The reverse if you hit left-handed.

Beyond the left field (schoolyard) fence was a narrow alley with a large garage immediately adjacent to the east. Then came a series of three flats extending east separated by narrow gangways. Early on, hitting the ball over the fence for a homer was a rare accomplishment. Within a few years, this feat became commonplace. Tony was the first to hit one over the fence into the alley. Larry was the first to hit it over the garage. As maturity set in, Tony, Larry, and Dale blasted the ball well into the gangways of the three flats. Memory serves that Terry and Carl were the last to hit a homer.

For some reasons known much later, the increase in power coincided with our increasing interest in the femme fatales at the time. America had Marilyn Monroe, Jane Mansfield, and Chicago's own and fellow Czech, Kim Novak. Foreign imports included Sophia Loren, Diana Dors, Brigitte Bardot, Anita Eckberg, Gina Lollobrigida, and Claudia Cardinale.

Larry prided himself as being the pitcher. Wearing a White Sox baseball cap, with the brim low, he took an elaborate wind up in which to fool us hitters. Unfortunately, throwing the ball for a strike was not his specialty. "Come on, Larry, get the ball over!" we implored. Because of his futility, we promptly nicknamed him Qualters after an equally inept pitcher on the 1958 White Sox named Tom Qualters.

Tony, Larry Prochaska, Carl in back.
Billy Coulson, Dale Bernard kneeling

Around the year 1998 or so, we had the occasion to meet Jim Landis and Pete Ward at breakfast before they attended an autograph show at the Rosemont Horizon. Jim was a star center fielder on the 1959 Sox American League championship team, and Pete was a star third baseman for the Sox in the 1960s. We asked them about Tom Qualters. They were amazed that we would remember such an obscure pitcher. We told them the story about nicknaming Larry to their great amusement.

One game that we will never forget was played on the south side of Sherlock. We only had four players, two on a side. Terry and Carl played Tony and another neighborhood friend, Gus Schultz. Terry pitched with all the determination we could only hope for from a current Cubs pitcher. He pitched a nine-inning no-hitter! We venture to say that this ranks as one of the greatest accomplishments ever in sports.

After many games, we stopped at Sully's mini store to buy some penny candy. Selections included small licorice discs made to resemble a 45 RPM record, candy buttons attached to a roll of paper, and miniature bottles made of wax and filled with sweet liquids. Every so often, we could afford a five-cents chocolate phosphate soda or a lime soda called a "green river". Has it really been sixty or so years since we enjoyed these delicacies?

About once a summer, we boys would clear our busy schedules to play a doubleheader, breaking only to have lunch at our respective homes. The grind of being a youngster!

We boys joined Little League teams with varying degrees of success. We played on the Cicero Braves team and developed the dreaded reputation of being "good field no hit" players. "Curveball, what is that?" We watched with awe as Jim M'lady bombed homers that seemed to fly the distance of those hit by our beloved Ernie Banks. Our mom and dad attended most games, attired in a house dress and business suit, respectively.

Carl, Tony

Little League

As teenagers, we began playing "swift pitch"—some say "fast pitch"—at Wilson School. With chalk, we drew the strike zone on the school wall. This game was usually played with two boys on each team. Pitches landing outside the drawn box were balls, while pitches taken by the batter which landed in the box were called strikes.

Sometimes we played one against one. We would each pick a major league team, announce the batter coming up to the plate, and swing righty or lefty depending on the particular player. We became fairly decent hitters.

For three weeks in August, our games were interrupted by our family vacation to Washington Island, on the tip of the thumb in Door County, Wisconsin.

We fondly remember our friends joining us in the annual ritual of picking nightcrawlers on the eve of our trips. This saved the expense of purchasing them on the island from the "worm lady", Carmen Lucke. We took pride in the fact that the inhabitants of the island considered our parents as islanders, not as tourists. Every year, the personnel operating the ferry greeted our parents with a sincere welcome back.

Not to be deterred, as baseball fans, we followed the island baseball team. The Islanders played in the Door County baseball league. The starting nine included Ray Hansen; Charlie Smith; Walter, Lonnie, Perry, and Kermit Jorgensen; Steve and Jake Ellefson; and Kirby Cornell.

Of course, we got to be friends with them all. Of course, we tried to fix-up the younger players with our sister Barbara.

The ballfield was on Main Road to the side of the Log Cabin Restaurant, which served great butterscotch sundaes. Practices were held once a week with games on Saturday. As we honed our skills, the players would let us join their practice. The players referred to us as Carl Yastrzemski and Tony Conigliaro. In 1961, when the Washington Senators moved to Minnesota and became the twins, the Islanders had us tell everyone that the "TC" on the Twins baseball cap stood for Tony and Carl, not the Twin Cities.

As the summer days got shorter and the air cooler, we kids began the process of transitioning to football. But first came the World Series!! During those years, baseball was dominated by the American League New York Yankees featuring Mickey Mantle, Yogi Berra, Whitey Ford, and Moose Skowron. As National League fans, we always rooted for the underdog.

It seems to defy reason that we got sick around this time of year. Having to stay home from school, we turned on the television and watched and listened to Mel Allen describe the action. This included watching Don Larsen's perfect game in 1956, six games of the 1957 series won by the Milwaukee Braves, and all seven games of the 1958 Series in which the Braves lost to the Yankees.

We remember sitting on our heads on the living room furniture, trying to change the luck of the Dodgers so they would get a hit off Don Larsen. We watched Hank Aaron, Red Schoendienst, Eddie Mathews, Warren Spahn, and Lew Burdette play for the Braves.

After the 1958 series, Red Schoendienst was hospitalized

with tuberculosis. At young ages, we both had become excellent artists, specializing in pencil portraits of our favorite sports players. We drew a portrait of Red and mailed it to him along with a letter encouraging him to get well, which we addressed to the hospital. We were overjoyed to receive a thank you letter from him shortly after that. Postmarked January 26, 1959, from St. Louis, it reads:

"Dear Tony and Carl:

Thanks for the nice letter and picture. Do you really think I look that good? Sure I will be playing again. Just keep watching.

Sincerely, Red Schoendienst".

```
Tony& Carl Ruzicka
5509 22nd Pl.
Cicero 50, Ill.

Dear Tony and Carl;

Thanks for the nice letter and picture.
Do you really think I looked that
good?

Sure I'll be playing again.  Just
keep watching.

                    Sincerely,

                    Red Schoendienst

RS:lw
```

As stated, it seemed our sickness at that time defied reason. Our walking into each and every rain puddle or dirt patch for a few weeks leading up to the Series certainly explains it to some degree. In 1957 we had the mumps. In 1958 the Asian Flu. Somehow, we recovered quickly after the completion of the Series.

Sadly, autumn set in, and we boys turned our attention to football. With the street mostly barren of cars, we played touch football on the street. The few cars that were parked were interwoven into our game plan. "Run to the blue Chevy and turn around for the pass . . . three steps to the Studebaker and then left . . . run to the old Buick, pause, then run out for a deep one!"

Sometimes we would play on Fifty-Fifth Avenue, being careful not to run on the lawn of Mrs. Zima, the widow of the corner shoemaker. If there was snow falling while delivering the *Cicero Life* on our morning paper route, we would shovel her snow. This fact, and her being a long-time acquaintance with our mom and dad, shielded us from her wrath. She would shake her fist at us boys, but secretly give an okay sign to us twins.

One day Terry Hrabak fell and chipped his front tooth. The dentist fixed him up, but his mom made him wear a football helmet even though we were playing touch football. As a symbol of solidarity, we all bought cheap helmets so that he would not feel uncomfortable. We painted C's on the side of our helmets to resemble the Bears helmets.

Our use of the helmets also gave comfort to our next-door neighbor Huey Stinnett who lived in 5511, the house where our father was born. Unfortunately, Huey was born with mental and physical challenges. As we graduated from 20-inch to 26-inch two-wheel bicycles, Huey rode a three-wheel bike and had to wear a helmet. That we were now also wearing helmets helped him feel less out of place.

Huey would wait at the fence separating our backyards, hoping to talk or play with us. Years later, when we went off to college, he told us that he, too, was in college. He was attending the Seguin School serving people with disabilities. To her everlasting credit, our mom made sure that we did not ignore Huey, although we admit that we often wished we could run right by him into our home. We believe that the lesson taught by our mom served us well when our careers led us to auditing non-profit organizations serving the underserved or disadvantaged.

We played tackle football on our front lawns with the sidewalks serving as end-zones. At that time, winters brought permanent snow cover, which softened our blows.

Other sports were also included in our play—soccer, basketball, street hockey. You name it, we played it! We played soccer on the street, no matter the season. One game on a Sunday night in December of 1958 stands out in our memory. Our father's brother, Uncle Stanley, died of a heart attack while driving on Cicero Avenue. Our father retrieved our uncle's car and parked it in front of our house. On that Sunday, we attended our uncle's wake. At age nine, we were intimidated, seeing him lying in the casket with shocking gray hair. As we played soccer that night, the ball rolled under our uncle's car. Dale, Larry, and Terry could not understand why we were reluctant to retrieve the ball as we were closest to it. We were deathly afraid that our uncle would pop up inside the car!

"Pinners" was a popular game. We would bang the ball against the front steps. Hitting the exact edge of the step would create a "pinner" with the ball flying far and true. If the ball landed on the front lawn of the house behind us on the other side of the street, it was a double. On the opposite sidewalk was a triple. Landing on the lawn adjacent to the opposite house was a home run. If you threw the ball and it missed the corner, this was a "goober". Three goobers made an out. We played one or two on a side.

At that time, our milk was delivered in glass bottles by the milkman, Al Mulak. Except for days when he had to collect money on his route and stop in for a cup of coffee, the milkman left the milk bottles on the porch near the front door. A few times, we would badly miss trying for a pinner, and the ball would bounce forward and break a bottle or two, with milk spilling out down the steps. Our mom was none too pleased! As adults, we learned that out east, they called this game "stoop ball". What fun!

One game was incorporated from watching on television: Jai alai! We all bought scoops, used a tennis ball, and played against the huge, metal warehouse door of the butcher store that was on the southside of Cermak Rd. The door was in the back alley near Alan and Dale Bernard's home. If you threw the ball just right you could hit the warehouse door and have it then bounce off the brick edge of the frame for a "rebolte"! We gave each other Hispanic sounding names and really enjoyed ourselves.

We played hide and go seek often. Friday nights we stopped our game for a few moments when we went inside and watched Norma, the sexy scoreboard girl, change the scores of the Cuban baseball game. Wow!

Another game was playing polo on our bicycles. The Oak Brook Polo Club played their matches in Oak Brook, a wealthy town about 5 miles west of us and right down Cermak Road. Our father would pack us into our 1959 Chevy, and we would have a wonderful Sunday afternoon watching the play.

One day our Uncle Bill came along, sitting in the backseat, crunched between us. The ticket taker assumed he was under twelve and gave him free admission. Perhaps this was the first time that we felt that being short had its advantages. We passed ourselves as around 5'5", Our father about 5'6", Tom about 5'7" and our mother and sister Barb even shorter. Years later, Tom confessed to only being 5'6". In separate parts of the room we both instantaneously said, "we used to look up to you!" We remained silent as to possible exaggeration of our height.

Oak Brook polo program

At the polo games we rubbed shoulders with the titans of industry: Paul Butler, president of Butler Paper Company, founder of Butler Aviation Company and founder of the town of Oak Brook; Russell Firestone of Firestone Tire; Billy Ylvisaker, CEO of Gould Inc.; Jim Kraml, owner of the Kraml Dairy which supplied the milk delivered to our doorstep; and Del Carroll, famous horse trainer. We, of course, got all their autographs.

The main attraction, however, was Cecil Smith, at that time America's only 10 goaler. As twins, we always had an advantage in meeting celebrities. Most were fascinated by how much we looked alike. We certainly used this to our advantage in approaching Cecil, and then countless celebs afterwards.

Polo is played with a long mallet and a wooden ball. When the ball went over the boards and out-of-play, fans could keep it. We often fought for the ball, seemingly just missing getting trampled by the thundering hoofs of the horses who could not stop at the boards. Some balls we took home for our game, others we had autographed by Cecil Smith and sold to fans for about one dollar! The players gave us mallets that had cracks and could not be used. With our bicycles serving as horses, we played some wonderful "chuckers"!

We developed a one- hole miniature golf course in our gangway. Alongside the neighbor's house was a strip of land, just east of our gangway sidewalk. We smoothed out the dirt and hammered an opened tin can into the turf for the hole. We were open for business! Taking our best knock- kneed stances, we gave our best imitations of Arnold Palmer. Even our parents enjoyed the game. As they came home from their various jobs, fathers would all try their hand at a hole-in-one before going into the house for dinner.

Other games included "it", "freeze tag" and "hopscotch". In 2006, when first courting his wife Qian Yi, Carl learned that she played the same games as a child in China.

The older boys, Alan Bernard, Alan Prochaska, and our brother Tom devised their own carnival, charging a 5 cents admission to go into the "horror chamber" or a few pennies to knock down milk bottles with a tennis ball. Our brother Tom would use the proceeds to buy a bleacher ticket to the Cubs games. The price was first 10 cents, slowly raised to 25 cents, and later 75 cents. We were outraged when sometime in the 1960's the price rose to a full dollar!

The carnival attempted to replicate the experiences at Riverview Amusement Park at Belmont and Western Avenues. A popular TV commercial promoting Riverview was one that featured Dick "Two Ton" Baker, who asked viewers to come to Riverview and "laugh your troubles away". Rides included the "Bobs", the "Shoot the Chute" and the "Rotor". Other features were "Aladdin's Castle" and the "Tunnel of Love".

Troubles? What troubles? We were too busy laughing to

notice. The weekly sounding of the air raid siren, deemed necessary because of the "Cold War" with the Soviet Union, and the occasional school mock air raid drill when we would seek shelter under our school desks did not temper our fun!

Television commercials enticed us to go to the Wisconsin Dells to experience the Tommy Bartlett Water Show. Instead, our parents took us to the Olson Rug Company on the corners of Pulaski and Diversey Avenues. Alongside the establishment was a small park complete with wooden Indians, teepees, a waterfall, and a wishing well. We told everyone that we were going to the "Bohemian Dells".

Although, not sports related, we kids would venture to the corner of Cermak and Central Avenues, stare at the sky pretending to see an object that did not exist and see how many people would stop and stare with us. A few times we brazenly stopped an elderly adult and asked if he or she would do us a favor. Bending down with our butt sticking out, we would ask them if they saw a hole in our pants!

Television shows included "Mighty Mouse", "Captain Midnight" and "Fury" on Saturday mornings. Also "Flash Gordon" serials which featured Buster Crabbe and were brought to us viewers by Larry Goodman, spokesman for Community Discount stores. We learned that Buster had been a gold medal winner in the 1932 Olympics. No wonder Flash always prevailed against "Ming the Merciless"!

We all watched westerns, such as the "Lone Ranger", "Tales of Wyatt Earp", "Gunsmoke", "Maverick", "Cheyenne", and "Shotgun Slade", starring Scott Brady. We all wore racoon skin caps just like Davy Crockett.

Situation comedies included "I Love Lucy", "My Little Margie", "Leave it to Beaver", "Father Knows Best", "Make Room for Daddy", and "Ozzie & Harriett". Ricky Nelson was introduced as the next heart throb, competing with Elvis Presley.

Each Sunday night we sat down with our parents to watch the Ed Sullivan Show.

Our parents listened to recordings of Frank Sinatra, Perry Como, Doris Day and Peggy Lee on the radio. Singing groups included The Four Lads and the Gaylords. Hit songs featured "High Hopes", "Me and My Shadow", "Ac-Cent-Tchu-Ate the Positive", "For Me and My Gal" , "Que Sera", "Secret Love", "Fever", "The Man I Love", "Moments to Remember", "Standing on the Corner", "From the Vine Came the Grape", and "Isle of Capri".

While us boys challenged our sister to rock with "Elvis the Pelvis" and sing along to "All Shook Up", "Hound Dog" and "Heartbreak Hotel", Barbara chose the melodies of Johnny Mathis: "Wonderful! Wonderful" and "Chances Are"; and Pat Boone: "April Love" and "Love Letters in the Sand". We did not realize at the time that she was nearing adulthood. We just figured that she grew tired of playing softball with us in our alley.

At various summer picnics, we had three legged and gunny sack races and played ball. Afterwards we would cool ourselves down. Reaching into a large tub filled with ice water, we would pull out a bottle of chocolate Kayo soda, or grape and orange crush Nehi sodas. This was followed up with cold, freshly cut watermelon. What a life!

Major League Baseball consisted of 16 teams, 8 in each of the National and American Leagues. The National Football League consisted of 14 teams, 7 each in the Western and Eastern Conferences. The National Hockey League consisted of 6 teams.

Besides for the players on the Chicago teams, it was easy to form attachments to other teams' players. We saw the visiting teams much more often than in today's games!

THE JOURNEY BEGINS

Carl, Bill Bishop, Tony

ONE SUMMER DAY IN 1960, at age eleven, we opened the sports page of our local newspaper. Inside was a picture of a football player in his spread-eagle position. Underneath the picture the caption read, "Bill Bishop, a resident of Cicero, gets ready to play for the Chicago Bears." We exclaimed: "Bill Bishop lives in Cicero?" We immediately went to our phone book to see if he was listed. There it was, not William Bishop, not W. Bishop, not B. Bishop, but Bill Bishop residing at 1842 S. 61st Ave.

Joined by Terry Hrabak, we rode our bikes a little over a mile to his home and rang the doorbell. It was answered by a slender young woman about our height, Marilyn Bishop, wife of Bill. "Is this the home of Bill Bishop of the Bears? Is he home? Can we speak to him?" we asked excitedly. She replied "This is his home, he is in, yes you can come in." Marilyn called Bill to the door and we proceeded to go downstairs to his den where he brought out his scrapbook and shared it with us. We had never been in the home of a professional athlete and it seemed like we were in heaven.

After peppering him with questions such as who is the hardest running back to tackle (his answer was Joe Perry fullback for the San Francisco 49ers), Bill mentioned that on that upcoming Saturday he was hosting a barbeque for some of the players and suggested we come with our autograph books. He then gave us each a picture of him in the Bears uniform along with a personalized autograph. We left his home ecstatic, looking forward to the upcoming barbeque with our minds racing as to what players we would meet. It seemed as if we had known Bill for years instead of the hour or so of this first meeting.

Saturday finally arrived. We went to the Bishop house at the earliest moment with autograph books in hand. The players began to arrive: Rick Casares, star fullback; Willie Galimore, star running back who happened to be black (In a recent visit to Marilyn Bishop, now 89 years old, she mentioned that Bill would call the Cicero police department to give them advance notice that he would have black visitors); Bill George, star middle linebacker and future Pro Football Hall of Famer; George Blanda, star quarterback who began his career with the Bears, claimed fame with the Houston Oilers and Oakland Raiders, and is in the Pro Football Hall of Fame; Ed Sprinkle, Pro Football Hall of Famer and retired Bear; Johnny Aveni, Bears place kicker; and Bob Konovksy, offensive lineman with the Chicago Cardinals. Bob was not much of a player, but had graduated from our high school, J. Sterling Morton East High School in Cicero. Other players were there too.

We suppose it was a combination of us being twins and of

our Bears knowledge, that led to us regaling these heroes with **our** stories. What a night!

We continued to visit Bill on a regular basis, although Terry never went back. At that time, a grass field existed at 19th and Lombard, just a few blocks from the Bishop home. We would practice our football skills while we waited for Bill's blue and white Buick to arrive in his driveway. Bill and Marilyn always welcomed us as did Marilyn's mother whom we called "Mrs. Petrik."

As youthful Chicago Bears fanatics and now personal friends with a member of the team, we truly began to follow the Bears and the National Football League (as well as the American Football League) in the 1960 season. We would follow every game closely, preparing a sheet to record Bill's exploits for that game. Each sheet was entitled "Bill Bishop, #73, defensive tackle, North Texas State University, along with the date and opponent of the game. There was a column for tackles and a column for assists. Unfortunately, Bill was nearing the end of his career. The stat sheet had few entries. If he so much as appeared on the TV screen, we marked it as a tackle with great laughter.

The following spring of 1961, we were saddened to learn that Bill was selected by the Minnesota Vikings in the dispersal draft forming that team. The sadness turned to elation when he was chosen to become the Vikings first defensive captain along with Don Joyce, formerly of the Baltimore Colts.

We continued our obsession with the Bears. We would take the "L" (Chicago's elevated train transit system) to Wrigley Field each Saturday of a home game to wait for the players to arrive for, and then exit from, their practice. We collected autographs and talked with the players and coaches.

This trip was one that we had often made going to Cubs games. We got on the train at the 54th Ave station, just behind Cermak Road on 21st street. This station was the beginning/end of the Douglas Park line (now the Pink Line). We transferred at

Jackson and walked under the tunnel to the Howard Ave line. Half of the ride was above ground, with the middle portion beneath. The Wrigley Field stop is Addison Street. As the train winds its way towards Addison, the Wrigley Field scoreboard appears. What a sight! To this day, it is hard to resist the urge to run as fast as possible to the field after exiting the train.

At that time, all teams were using the T Formation in which the quarterback takes the snap directly from the center. The T Formation was modernized by Clark Shaughnessy when he was the head football coach at Stanford University. Mr. Shaughnessy, then head football coach at the University of Chicago (yes, they had a football team!), approached George Halas with the concept in 1935.

In 1961, the San Francisco 49ers were the first team to revert to the Shotgun Formation in which the quarterback stands well behind the center, approximately 7 yards, to receive the snap. The 49ers coach, Jim "Red" Hickey implemented the Shotgun, and, in a further tweak, rotated quarterbacks. John Brody primarily passed, Billy Kilmer primarily ran, and Bobby Waters did both. In the first five games of the 1961 season, the 49ers won 4 and lost 1 and averaged 33 points per game. In games three through five, they went undefeated and averaged 41 points.

The Bears were to play them in game six on October 22, 1961. The preceding Thursday, October 19, 1961, "Sports Illustrated" magazine included an article on the 49ers and the shotgun. The article included details of the formation. As eager 6th graders, we decided to help the Bears with their defense! We sat at the kitchen table with pencil and tablet paper and came up with our solution. We studiously recorded it on the paper and two days later we went to Wrigley Field, sitting outside the firehouse on Waveland Avenue, waiting for the players and coaches.

Clark Shaughnessy was now the Defensive Coordinator for the Bears. As he left the park, we excitedly approached him. "Clark, what are you going to do to stop the shotgun?" we asked.

He replied, "I have it right here boys", pointing to charts under his arm. "Please let us see", we responded. "The game is tomorrow, and I can't let you see", he replied. "There are no bigger Bears fans than us, please show it to us", we retorted. With a sigh Clark relented, "OK, here is the chart!" He showed us the detailed defensive formation to be put into place for the game.

Taking our paper out of his pocket, Tony exclaimed "that is exactly what we came up with!!" Coach Shaughnessy and the Ruzicka twins had both designed a defense that had Bill George, the Bears middle linebacker, line up directly in front of San Francisco's center, who having to hike the ball several yards between his legs, was not well positioned to block. The Bears did not allow a point while shutting out San Francisco 31-0. Later when we were clubhouse boys, we learned many of the Bears offensive formations and were not shy of suggesting plays to Coach Halas.

At this time, we had never been to a Chicago Bears game, although we had often gone by ourselves to Cubs games and Bears practices. The tickets were too expensive and hard to come by. As luck would have it (we like to think that luck has always been on our side), we were approached by Mr. Matusek, a member of our church, the Warren Park Presbyterian Church in Cicero. He was offering us his two tickets for that day's game. It happened to be the last game of the year and the Bears were playing the Vikings! We could go to our first game and see Bill! What good fortune! We hurried home, changed into warm clothes, and hurried to the "L".

The Bears won the game 52-35 and Bill hardly played. Yet, we hurried down the stairs to the concourse to see if we could see Bill as he made his way to the visitor clubhouse. Success! Approaching, separated by metal bars, Bill told us that he had an autograph football for us and that he would be returning home later in the week. We walked by his house each day, hoping to see his car once again appear in the driveway.

What a bonanza! We were presented with the ball, autographed by the entire Viking team, including Pro Football Hall of Fame members Coach Norm Van Brocklin, Fran Tarkenton, and Hugh McElhenney.

Also signing the ball was Jim Marshall, a member of the famed "Purple People Eaters" who notoriously picked up an opponent's fumble and ran 66 yards the wrong way for what he thought was a touchdown. He threw the ball up in celebration, but soon realized his run had resulted in a two-point safety for the opponent.

Tony's daughter- in-law, Clara, is from Minnesota, and is impressed with this coup.

We were so happy! As we walked home down Cermak Road, we could not resist the urge to throw the ball to each other. "Careful, we don't want to ruin the autographs."

In 7th and 8th grade. John (Lonnie) Larsen and we were members of the church's basketball team. None of us were very skilled, especially John. He had painted his basketball red, white, and blue, just as the balls used by the Harlem Globetrotters. A teammate nicknamed him "Lonnie Meadowlarse", after Meadowlark Lemon. In high school, John joined other members of our church, Chuck Soumar and Bob Bergland, in teaming up with Jim Peterik from Morton West High School to form the Ides of March rock in roll band.

During our many trips to Wrigley Field, we befriended Andy Frain. Jr. and Mike Frain, sons of Andy Frain, who had started the famed usher services. Mike allowed us to sneak into the 1961 College All Star Football Game. It was there that we secured the autograph of Ben Davidson. At 6'8" and 275 lbs., Ben was one of football's biggest players. In getting the autograph, Ben stepped on Carl's foot, with cleats and all. It was worth the price of the autograph. Ben went on to star for the Oakland Raiders and in "Miller Lite" beer ads with John Madden and Rodney Dangerfield.

At one of our many visits, sometime in early 1962, Marilyn

Bishop suggested we write George Halas asking if we could be clubhouse boys for the Bears for their upcoming season. We did so, emphasizing our friendship with Bill and Marilyn Bishop, our loyalty to the Bears, and our excellent grades in school. On July 2, 1962, Coach Halas wrote us the following letter:

"Dear Carl and Tony

I received your nice letter inquiring as to a job as clubhouse boys for this season. It was mighty nice of Mrs. Bill Bishop to suggest you write to me, but I am sorry to tell you that it will not be possible as we will have the same boys as last year.

I was really pleased to hear that you were on the school's golden Honor Roll all three semesters, and if you do this again next year, we will certainly make every effort to take you on the following season. I will speak to Ed Rozy, our trainer, who is in charge of our clubhouse.

With best wishes, I am sincerely yours.

Geo. S. Halas"

It is difficult to fully relay our excitement. George Halas, one of the founding fathers of the National Football League, owner and coach of our beloved Chicago Bears wrote us back and we may have the job the next year!

We now had greater incentive to succeed in school, although the most overriding incentive was always to make our parents proud. We maintained our Golden Honor Roll status and following Coach Halas' instructions, wrote him again the following spring.

In May 1963, near the end of 8th grade, we received the following letter dated May 18, 1963:

"Dear Carl and Tony:

Your letter came while I was away on vacation and since I have returned it has taken me quite a bit of time to get caught up with my correspondence.

I am certainly pleased to know that you have maintained your Honor Roll status, This is really fine news and I am sure that your parents are proud of you.

We will be glad to have your help as Club House boys this year. Of course, we will have a regular boy for Monday through Friday. However, On Saturdays and Sundays we will be glad to have your help.

I suggest that you call our trainer, Ed Rozy, so that he can give you the information concerning the details.

Looking forward to having you with us and with all good wishes, I am

Sincerely yours, Geo. S. Halas"

This letter affected our future in so many positive ways: successful high school running; Yale University; University of Chicago Graduate School of Business; lifetime friendship with Frank Shorter, Yale teammate and Gold and Silver medal winner in the 1972 and 1976 Olympic marathons; living in Glencoe; becoming founders of the Chicago Marathon; and our friendship with Yosh Kawano, long time clubhouse manager of the Chicago Cubs. For this we are eternally grateful to Marilyn Bishop.

We began turning our radio dial to stations that played "The Twist" by Chubby Checker", "Soldier Boy" by the Shirelles, and "The Duke of Earl", by Gene Chandler.

THE JOURNEY
CONTINUES

W

HO WOULD HAVE THOUGHT THE "Cicero Life" sports page could be so wonderfully influential in our fairy tale childhood? One winter Sunday in 1962, we again opened its pages to see a picture of Pierre Pilote, star Chicago Blackhawks defenseman and captain of the team that had just won the Stanley Cup in 1961. The picture stated that he was a resident of Berwyn, the town just west of Cicero. Once again, we tried our luck with the phone book. Again success! The listing read: P. Pilote 2813 S. Ridgeland Ave.

As it was cold and snowy, rather than ride our bikes, we walked the roughly two miles to this residence. The refrain mirrored that of our first encounter with Bill Bishop. Ringing the doorbell, we were greeted by Mrs. Pilote: "Is this the home of Pierre Pilote of the Blackhawks? Is he home? Can we speak to him?" Having answered in the affirmative to our excited inquiries, she invited us in. Pierre spent about a half hour with us and gave us each a personalized autographed picture postcard.

While there was no Saturday evening barbeque like with the Bears and Bill Bishop, we still hit the jackpot. As we were ready to leave, Pierre asked us if we would like to meet Glenn Hall, the Blackhawks goalie who lived nearby. "Mr. Goalie? Glenn Hall? Of course!"

First Pierre called Glenn as to make sure we would be welcomed, as Glenn took a nap before each game. After being told that Glenn would love to see us, we were given his address: 3212 S. Gunderson Ave. Off we went on another exciting journey. Again, we were each given a personalized autographed picture postcard. Both Pierre Pilote and Glenn Hall are in the Hockey Hall of Fame. The NHL television network recently voted Glenn Hall's 502 consecutive game streak as goalie as the 2nd most record that will never be broken.

We had hit upon a gold mine. Many of the Hawks lived in south Berwyn and we were given new addresses each time we met a player. The chain went something like this: Pierre Pilote, Glenn Hall, Stan Mikita, Bobby Hull, Gerry Melnyk, Len Lunde, and then the most treasure friend of them all, Chico Maki residing at 3622 S. Elmwood Ave.

Chico Maki, #16, right-wing for the Chicago Blackhawks. He was such a wonderful friend. He and his wife Nancy welcomed us to their home on a regular basis. Sports at that time had not exploded in popularity with astronomical player salaries. Chico and Nancy lived in the upstairs living space of a bungalow owned by Mr. and Mrs. Maid and paid rent of $100 per month. Later, Chico felt it was only fair to volunteer $150 per month payment. We would go around to the back of the house, ring the doorbell, and Chico would come down the backstairs to let us in.

The living quarters consisted of a small back porch with the back stairwell, then a door leading into the living quarters: a fairly large kitchen, a small living room, tiny bath, and two bedrooms towards the front of the house. We mostly came unannounced, yet, were never turned away. Upon reflection, it seems unbelievable! We all sat around the kitchen table. We discussed the Blackhawks, school (first grade school, then high school, followed by college and graduate school), the Bears, the Cubs, our running. Everything!

At that time, Bobby Hull and Stan Mikita, both members of the Hockey Hall of Fame, were the stars of the team. Chico played on the "HEM" line: Bobby Hull on left wing, Phil Esposito at center and Chico Maki on right wing. Bobby was the Michael Jordon of his day. Bobby signed every autograph, gave every interview, and became only the third player in the NHL (National Hockey League) history to score 50 goals in a season. He went on to record five 50 goal seasons. Bobby's wrist shot was timed at 118 miles per hour.

Chico assisted on many of Bobby's goals and played stellar defense. A frequent discussion around the kitchen table was us imploring Chico, "You should shoot more!" After all, he once scored 41 goals in the minors. Chico replied. "why shoot a pop-gun when you can shoot a cannon."

Each morning after a Blackhawks game we would stop at the corner store on our way to school and look in the back Sports section of the Chicago Sun Times for the statistics of the game. If the Hawks won and Chico did not score a goal or get an assist, we were disappointed. If they lost, but he had a few points, we were happy.

Throughout later years, we would occasionally see Stan Mikita. Once we asked him, "who was a better hockey player, Chico Maki or Cliff Koroll?" Cliff played on a line with Stan and scored more goals than Chico, but we felt was not as good an all-around player. Stan always evaded answering.

Around 2005 or so, we had an occasion to be with Jim Pappin, an ex- Blackhawk winger, and asked the same question. Jim responded: "Billy Reay (coach of the Hawks) would not trade Chico Maki for two Cliff Korolls"! Even though we were now in our 50's it is hard to describe the electricity flowing through our bodies. Chico was the man!

One day, Chico called and said he had something for us. Excitedly, we raced to the house and rang the back bell. In his hand was a Blackhawk directory, complete with players' addresses and phone numbers. As copying machines were not yet the norm, we took the directory home and typed a copy.

In 2013, Tony went to the Cicero Public Library to do a search through the archives for the photographs of Bill Bishop and Pierre Pilote that had influenced our lives. It was a very tedious process as he advanced through years of old film of the newspaper. While not exactly successful, he did find newspaper articles that not only told which Blackhawks players lived in Berwyn, but also gave each player's home address. It was most definitely a different time.

One day we visited Bobby Hull who had moved to an apartment in Hillside. Many of the Hawks lived in the complex: Elmer Vasko, Al MacNeil, Wayne Hillman, and others. Bobby enjoyed us playing with his son of about one year of age. This little baby was Brett Hull who also became a 50-goal scorer in five different seasons and an NHL hall of famer! Who knew?

Bobby Hull Drawing

Chico Maki Drawing

In April 1963, we rode our bikes to Stan Mikita and Jill Cerny's wedding. Jill was a classmate of our sister Barbara and the daughter of friends our parents knew from the "Czech Odd Fellows Club." Members of the wedding party included Glenn Hall, Mike Ditka of the Bears, and Mickey Madigan, a local insurance agent. The fans swarmed outside the church, mostly to get a glimpse of Bobby Hull.

Another time Chico called us to come to his home after school as he had something for us. He had brought home some curved blade sticks of Bobby Hull and Stan Mikita. This was their invention that became the rage of hockey. Later the league outlawed the extreme curve and legislated the curve's legal dimensions. We used the sticks playing pickup games, street hockey and hockey on the hardwood floors of our rooms at Yale! Somehow, Chico sensed when our sticks were becoming too whittled down to be of any use and called us to pick up another supply.

Blackhawks tickets were expensive and hard to get. Once or twice a year, Chico would call and say he had tickets for us. He would pick us up and drop us off at our home. As we made our way northeast on Ogden Ave to the stadium, sitting in the back seat with Chico driving and Nancy alongside, we knew that we were privileged twins. After the game, we had to wait for Chico to shower and sign autographs.

In the concourse, he would occasionally introduce us to rival players that he had played with in the minors. Dicky Duff of Toronto and Vic Hatfield of New York come to mind as players we met. Years later, via phone, Chico told us that fraternizing with a rival was forbidden. He was afraid to do so even in the off season, fearing that he would suffer repercussions from Hawk management. "Why then did you introduce us to Dicky Duff, Vic Hatfield, and others?", we asked. He replied, "You guys were always special!"

One game, Chico's mother was visiting from Canada and the five of us made the trip to the stadium. She sat with Nancy in the player's family section, while we sat in the second balcony. During the game, the usually mild- mannered Chico got into a fight with Doug Barkley, a defenseman for the Detroit Red Wings who was one of the biggest players at that time. We were fearful for Chico while waiting for him to come out of the locker room. His mother will really admonish him. Upon coming out, Chico's mother proclaimed: "I was never so proud of you in my life, Chico!" We all laughed.

All home games were not televised, and correspondingly, there were no TV timeouts. Chico dropped us off at our house around 10:20 PM, just in time to see the replays on the evening news. Today the game finishes about that time.

The Blackhawk hockey program, "Chicago Stadium Review"

cost 25 cents. Advertisements included car rental for $5 per day plus 5 cents a mile and hotel room rental for $4.50 per night.

With our fondness for football, we would carry a football around with us just about everywhere we went. One Saturday we visited Chico, with football in hand. Also visiting him was Phil Esposito (a future Hockey Hall of Fame member); Dennis De Jordy, the Hawks backup goalie; and Murray Hall, a seldom used winger. They wanted to play football, so we went to the playground at 28th and East Ave. They were no match for the mighty Ruzicka twins as we found out that their hockey skills did not translate to another sport!

We would always ask Chico to play hockey with us at the frozen, flooded playground. It was not far from his house. He always politely refused. But one day Chico called: "My skates are at the stadium, but if you have skates for me, I will meet you there!" We were excited: "Great, what size skate do you wear, 9 or 9 ½?" He told us that he wore a size 6 ½ skate which we disappointedly could not produce. This was when we learned that skaters use skates smaller than their regular shoe size, as opposed to us kids having skates larger because we would eventually "grow into them."

For years prior to his death in August 2015, Chico suffered from numbness and tingling in his feet. He believed that it was due to an injury when checked violently against the boards. We always wondered if such a small size skate had anything to do with it.

Years later, around 2005 or so, Tony and Yosh Kawano were shopping at the Dominick's (now Mariano's) grocery on Willow near our office in Northfield. Seeing a huge line, he discovered that Bobby Hull was signing autographs. Tony called Carl to hurry and meet him there. We had not seen Bobby since we were about 20 years old, or for a span of 36 years. Upon seeing the two of us, Bobby was ecstatic! "Oh my God it's the twins! Remember when you guys helped push my car out of the driveway on Wenonah? Remember when you guys were bouncing Brett on your laps? Do you hear from George Meyers?" Wow, we had made a lifetime impression on such a star, just like he had made one on us!

We often saw Stan Mikita practicing golf at the White Pines Golf Dome in Bensenville. In 1985 the Blackhawks had an exciting season. Tony told Stan that it was fun watching hockey again. Stan told Tony, "It's a much different game now. The players are much bigger and faster. We would have a difficult time if we played in today's game." Tony replied, "Speak for yourself Stan!"

In 1999, Tony and his family traveled to Prague in the Czech Republic. Stan was born in Sokoice in the Slovak Republic. Carl told Stan about the trip. Stan was excited, but told Carl that he was Slovak, not Czech. Carl replied, "You're still a pretty nice guy, Stan!"

At Stan Mikita's memorial service at the United Center, Bobby saw us and insisted that we meet him after paying our respects to Jill and the Mikita family. We still call Bobby every month or so to see how he is doing.

The only person we took to visit Chico was our nephew, Mike. He was interested in hockey, while his younger brother, Matt, was too little and had little interest in being out in the cold. We would all ice skate on a frozen pond. Matt did not want to leave the car, so we told him to just beep his horn when he wanted us to come back to him. We would barely have finished lacing up our skates when the horn would blow.

Ultimately, Chico and Nancy had three sons: Michael, Stephen, and Jimmy. They all happily survived in their small living quarters. Michael is now an air traffic controller in Toronto, Stephen a pilot for Jet Blue Airlines based in Orlando, Florida and Jimmy is an appraiser in Simcoe, Ontario. Chico and Nancy ultimately divorced, but we stayed in touch with each of them.

We last saw Chico in 1980 when we travelled to Buffalo

to cheer Frank Shorter in the American trials for the Olympic marathon. We stayed overnight at his home in Simcoe, Ontario the night prior to the race.

Frank performed miserably. At the 25- mile mark, he asked us if he was ahead of a certain runner from Colorado. We assured him that he was. This is one of many times that the three of us uttered "thank God for life's little victories". Frank was so depressed that he considered driving back with us to Chicago, rather than flying back to Colorado with his wife Louise and son Alex.

We stayed in touch with Chico by phone until his death. We take pride in the fact that we were instrumental in having the Hawks send him a 2010 Stanley Cup Champion ring. A few years later, we would also secure a championship ring for another friend involved in a different sport.

Sadly, at the end of every season, Chico and family would return to Canada. In early September as training for the new season began, we would ride our bikes to Chico's house hoping for his return. We would ride for hours around the nearby blocks, circling around, ever observant. No luck. "Let's circle around one more time, do you want to go home? Maybe one more trip around the block." As we circled for the umpteenth time, we saw a wonderful sight: a car parked in front of his house with a Canadian license plate! Another season of joy and happiness was about to begin!

We were now listening to "He's so Fine", by the Cliftons; "Walk Right In", by The Rooftop Singers; and It's My Party", by Leslie Gore.

As Chico left for Canada in 1963, a new journey was about to begin for the Ruzicka twins!

WELCOME TO THE CHICAGO BEARS

173 WEST MADISON STREET • CHICAGO 2, ILLINOIS

May 18, 1963

PHONE DEarborn 2-5400

Messrs. Carl and Tony Ruzicka
5509 West 22nd Place
Cicero 50, Illinois

Dear Carl and Tony:

Your letter came while I was away on vacation and since I have
returned, it has taken me quite a bit of time to get caught up with
my correspondence.

I am certainly pleased to know that you have maintained your Honor Roll
status.   This is really fine news and I am sure that your parents are
proud of you.

We will be glad to have your help as Club House boys this year.   Of
course, we will have to have a regular boy for Monday through Friday.
However, on Saturdays and Sundays we will be glad to have your help.

I suggest that you call our trainer, Ed Rozy, so that he can give you
the information concerning the details.

Looking forward to having you with us and with all good wishes, I am

Sincerely yours,

George Halas

Geo. S. Halas

GSH:o

Letter from George Halas

THE CHICAGO BEARS PLAYED IN Wrigley Field during our years as Clubhouse Boys, 1963-1966. Because the Chicago Cubs ending season and the Chicago Bears beginning season coincided, the first three Bears games of each season were away games. The Cubs and Bears used the same clubhouse, thus while we were moving the Bears equipment in, the Cubs were moving their equipment out. That is how we had the good fortune to meet longtime Cubs equipment and clubhouse manager, Yosh Kawano. "Hey twins, move that box", he ordered. "Yes sir, Mr. Kawano", we replied. Later we became the closest of friends.

We worked the Saturday before the game and then game day on Sunday. On Saturdays there were offensive and defensive meetings in the clubhouse which were followed by a brief practice on the field with the players just in their sweat clothes. Our job was to make sure the players had their equipment for practice, keep track of the balls, tend to the players' needs, pick up their clothing after practice and take it to the laundry, generally clean the clubhouse, and then set up the player's lockers for gameday.

To understand how small and tight these quarters were, the Bears (and Cubs) clubhouse is now used by the Wrigley Field ground crew. The door to the clubhouse was just inside the park from Waveland Avenue. The exit onto the field was at the far corner of the left field wall. When entering the clubhouse, the first floor was where the coaches and Mr. Halas had quarters. When turning left toward the field and down a few steps, the washroom and showers were to the left and the training room was to the right. Between these areas there were two sinks with a mirror and shelf. On the shelf were two glass jars with a piece of adhesive tape serving as a label marked "pep pills." One jar had red pills. The other jar's pills were green. A player would ask, "Hey twin, get me two reds and a green". Another player requested "two greens and a red." It was only in later years that we realized that we had been welcomed to the world of "uppers and downers" and PED's, (performance enhancing drugs).

There were two toilets and two urinals and six showers, not much for a 40 men roster and 8 or 9 coaches. Continuing toward the field and down a few steps were the players' lockers, which surrounded the walls of the rectangular room.

We can still visualize the location of each player's locker. Although mostly assigned by number, there were a few exceptions. We remember how the clubhouse came to life with the entrants of player after player, getting ready for practice or gameday. We can still smell the aroma of analgesic and freshly cut oranges. We can vividly recall the pre practice chatter, replaced by the pre- game silence as the players made their final preparations. We remember how injured players became non-entities to the coaches. They were of no use for the game on hand.

The equipment was maintained at the very east end of the clubhouse directly under the box seats. There was only one door to this room (in the middle between two lockers) and there were no windows. Just as the box seats slope down to the field, so did the ceiling of the equipment room. We would joke that we were hired for the job because we were only 5'5"! Then again, Yosh Kawano pushed 5'at best.

When disrobing, pretty much every player just dropped their socks, undershirts, uniform tops and pants, jock straps, etc. on the floor. When they wiped themselves after showering, the towels also made it to the floor. Our job included picking up the laundry from the floor, sorting it into laundry tubs with uniforms (after we removed knee, thigh and hip pads on game days) placed in one basket, under clothing (t-shirts and jock straps) placed in a second basket, and towels in another. We also removed each player's belt from their pants and hung it in their respective locker for game day.

We would then take the laundry to White Bear Laundry a block north on Clark Street. We later learned that this laundry was owned by Coach Halas. Just like our father's stepmom renting out the main residence while living in the small garden apartment, Coach Halas was true to his Czech heritage in finding ways to both save and make money.

We would then sweep and mop the floors making sure everything was clean for game day. On Saturday we would also arrange each player's locker for game day. Each helmet was hung on a hook that protruded from the side of the locker. Established procedure was to place a t-shirt on the top of the helmet, with a jockstrap placed on top of the t-shirt. We then hung their game day jerseys and pants on a rod that extended across the top of each locker. Lastly, we polished the shoes so they would be shiny for the game.

Our senior year of high school, we each took a class in psychology. As an experiment of the human mind affecting behavior, we decided to do something different. We decided to put the jockstrap on first and the t-shirt next. Pretty much every player yelled that they did not have a jock strap. We would lead them by the hand, removing the t-shirt, thus revealing the jockstrap.

As stated, on Saturdays, before the brief on-field practice, the defensive team would meet in the player locker room space and the head defensive coach, George Allen (Pro Football Hall of Fame) would show film of the opponent's offense from their previous game(s). The coaches and players would discuss movements of various players, various formations and what that meant about the play that was happening. The offensive players and coaches met on the top floor, outside of Coach Halas and the other coaches' quarters, where they would go over the films of the opponent's defense.

Our job on gameday before the game was to make sure all players had their equipment, cut up oranges for half time consumption, clean and/or change spikes after a brief pregame on-field practice and, inflate the footballs to the 13 lbs. per square inch requirement.

Most avid followers of the NFL now know about "Deflategate" involving the allegation that Tom Brady, star quarterback of the New England Patriots, requested that deflated footballs be used in the 2014 American Football Conference Championship game. It is our memory that we inflated approximately 15 balls before each game to the regulated 13 lbs. per square inch of air pressure. We each have distinct memory that was the perfect inflation. Less or more made the ball too spongy or too hard making it harder for us to throw and catch the ball.

Before the game started one of the referees would come to the clubhouse and, using a gauge, spot test a few footballs, and then take one ball to start the game. All others were kept in the bag and taken out by Tony should he have to throw his spare into play, primarily when the ball was kicked into the stands. There was absolutely no oversite should we change balls, get a different bag from the clubhouse once the game started, etc. Additionally, the balls we provided were the only game balls. The opposing team did not have their own supply.

Tony was told to do whatever he could to make sure a ball did not go into the stands. After the 1965 season when Gale Sayers scored so many touchdowns, there was a newspaper article informing the public about how many balls were lost during the season and its negative financial impact on the Bears. In 1973 before graduating from the University of Chicago Graduate School of Business, Tony interned on the accounting and audit staff of Arthur Young & Company. He was on the team performing the audit of Wilson Sporting Goods, maker of the official NFL Duke footballs. He learned that each NFL team received 250 free footballs annually from Wilson as a promotional item. Negative financial impact involving free footballs?

Before each game, one fan sitting in the leftfield corner box seat area that was later made famous by the Cubs "Bartman game", always wanted us to throw a ball to him and he would throw it back to us on the field. This became a good luck ritual.

The four years of work went by quickly. On our final game, we threw the fan the ball and told him to keep it. "Sorry Coach".

During the game, Tony followed the line of scrimmage with a spare ball, while Carl made sure the players' spikes were cleaned and that the players all had jackets or parkas to keep warm. Carl also made numerous trips to the clubhouse for items a player would request.

Because the Cubs were finishing up their season schedule, the first three games of the 1963 season were away games, with the first played on September 15th at Green Bay. Working only the weekends of home games, our job had not yet begun. We found out that the Bears were going to have an early morning practice on Saturday at Soldier Field before traveling to Green Bay. Excitedly, but timidly, we went to the practice. Having no official credentials as clubhouse boys, we talked our way into the field.

In our 4 years working, we never had credentials of any sort. This became problematical when Joe Marconi, Bears fullback, would ask Carl to get some pastry at the bakery on Addison and Sheffield. Not sure that the ushers would recognize him and let him back into the park, Carl made sure he told the attending usher to please stay put, so he would be recognized and allowed to return without difficulty. We even had difficulty getting into the gate manned by Coach Halas' brother, Frank!

We waited anxiously for the players to come out for practice. The first to appear were Roosevelt Taylor and Bennie McRae, members of the defensive backfield. We mustered up enough courage to start a conversation. They asked, "where are you from? What are you doing here?". They then uttered magical words, "We look forward to seeing you at Wrigley". This was unbelievable! We will really get to know our heroes!

The first home game of the 1963 was Sunday October 6th against the Baltimore Colts. On the Saturday prior, we reported to work. Our immediate boss was Bill Martell, who served as the head of the clubhouse. As he explained our duties, we somewhat intrepidly waited for the players to appear. As you faced towards the clubhouse from our equipment room door, the first locker on the left was used by Bill George. He greeted us warmly. We are sure that within not too short of a time, we let him know of our defensive scheme for beating the 49ers shotgun in 1961!

The Bears won the game 10-3 which made them 4 and 0 for the start of the season. Our memory is that defensive tackle Stan Jones was awarded the game ball. It was then that we learned the song accompanying the presentation. Coach Halas would gather the team in the clubhouse immediately after the game, announce the winner, and present the ball to the winner. This was followed by all team members singing "Hurray for Stan. Hurray at last. Hurray for Stan. He's a horses a_ _."

During this game we learned that Coach Halas often had a swearing vocabulary when yelling at the referees during the game. Growing up, our parents and certainly our uncles often used swear words. However, certain of those considered the worst were never spoken. These were the words most prevalent in the Coach's vocabulary. When we first heard Coach Halas swearing at an official, our immediate reaction was to fear that if our mother found out, she would prohibit us from working. Later in the game, Tony was standing next to Coach Halas when he heard the same words. They were not coming from Coach Halas and there were no coaches or players that were close by. Tony learned that the words were coming from the Bears mascot! Is nothing sacred?

Coach Halas was not allowed past the 50 yard-line, while Tony followed the entire line of scrimmage. When Tony was on the Bears' side of the 50 yard-line, Coach Halas often kneeled next to Tony resting his arm on Tony's knee or shoulder. This, too, was unbelievable!

Carl, George Halas, Tony

President John F. Kennedy was assassinated on Friday, November 22, 1963. Two days later, the Bears played the Pittsburgh Steelers in Pittsburgh. NFL commissioner, Pete Rozelle, decided that the game would be played without television or radio coverage. Unfortunately, we are ashamed to admit that we were upset. The Bears tied the Steelers thanks to a legendary catch and run by Mike Ditka. The Bears returned home the following weekend and played to another tie with the Vikings. We do not remember any discussion about the tragic event in the Bears locker room.

Rather than rehash each game, we have decided to relay highlights of our experiences:

The 1963 Bears won the NFL Championship. The Ruzicka twins had brought them luck. The game was played on a very cold December 29, 1963. The real temperature was 4 degrees with a windchill of minus 11. The Bears defense dominated the game, intercepting 5 passes. Key interceptions resulted in the

Bears two touchdowns, runs of 2 and 1 yards by quarterback Billy Wade. Larry Morris, right linebacker intercepted Y.A. Tittle in the 1st quarter, returning the ball 61 yards. Larry autographed our "Halas By Halas" book, writing "Thanks for all favors".

1963 Bears Championship autographed program

Ed O'Bradovich grew up in nearby Hillside, IL and graduated from fellow suburban league high school, Proviso East. In the 3rd quarter he intercepted a Tittle pass deep in Bears territory resulting in Billy Wade's winning quarterback sneak. Our fondest memory of Ed is how meticulously he dressed after the games. He went over his suit with a lint roller before departing the clubhouse. Our grandmother loved Ed and Rudy Bukich, back up quarterback, as they were of Croatian heritage. She was not interested in football, yet she knew their collegiate backgrounds and current statistics.

George Allen, defensive coach was awarded the game ball. Now more confident, we sang along, "Hurray for George. Hurray at last. Hurray for George. He's a horses a_ _."

If we listen closely, we can still hear Mike Ditka's good luck song, "Dominique" playing on the radio above Doug Atkin's locker. The artist was The Singing Nun. The championship, after all, seemed like a religious experience.

At their Saturday pre-game practice, we managed to get the autographs of certain New York Giants players who became members of the Pro Football Hall of Fame. These players were Frank Gifford, star halfback and first color commentator for "Monday Night Football"; Y.A. Title, star quarterback; and Sam Huff, star middle linebacker.

Each player's share of the championship money was $5900. Many of our friends thought that was how we were able to afford Yale. In fact, our tuitions were met via a combination of gift scholarship, loans, bursar jobs, and family contributions. For our efforts for the championship game we received about $50 in tips.

One of Tony's prize possessions is a picture of himself holding the ball standing next to Coach Halas near the end of the championship game. Tony is immortalized at Soldier Field as this picture is part of the permanent "Bears by the Decade" display in the Field's west concourse and can be found on the Bears' website.

Carl has kept a picture from the Tribune which features Coach Allen discussing strategy with Richie Petitbon, Joe Fortunato, and Larry Morris. He is in the foreground, kneeling and "prepared for action".

Often in later years, we would test the memories of our friends Yosh Kawano, Tom Gindorff and Paul Palandri by reliving the field announcement of the 1963 starting lineups, waiting for them to fill in the last name:

Offense: "at guard from Indiana, # 67, Ted Karras; at the other guard from Syracuse, #60, Roger Davis; at tackle from Notre Dame, # 63, Bob Wetoska; at the other tackle from Florida A&M University, # 70, Herman Lee; at center from Yale, # 50, Mike Pyle; at tight end from the University of Pittsburgh, # 89, Mike Ditka; At flanker from the University of California-Santa Barbara, # 47, Johnny Morris, at wide receiver from Prairie View A&M, #84, John "Bo" Farrington; at halfback from Florida A&M, # 28, Willie Galimore; at fullback from West Virginia, # 34, Joe Marconi; and at quarterback from Vanderbilt, # 9, Billy Wade."

Defense: "at tackle, from Arkansas, # 75, Fred Williams; at the other tackle, from Maryland, # 78, Stan Jones; at defensive end, from Tennessee, #81, Doug Atkins; at the other end, from Illinois, #87, Ed O' Bradovich; at outside linebacker, from Mississippi, #31, Joe Fortunato; at the other outside linebacker, from Georgia, #33, Larry Morris; at middle linebacker from Wake Forest, #61, Bill George; at cornerback from Michigan, #26, Bennie McRae; at the other cornerback, from Indiana, #23, Dave Whitsell; at strong safety, from Tulane, #17, Richie Petitbon; and at free safety, from Grambling, #24, Roosevelt Taylor."

Not to be left out, we added another announcement that we

never heard from the loudspeaker: "and in the clubhouse, from Cicero, Illinois, Tony and Carl Ruzicka!"

Rick Casares drawing

Dave Whitsell drawing

The games were broadcast over WGN radio, with Jack Brickhouse doing play by play and Irv Kupcinet doing the color commentary. Irv played briefly for the Philadelphia Eagles, but was famed for writing his daily "Kup's Column" for the Chicago

Sun Times (where he would report on the celebrity scene) and hosting his own syndicated television show on Saturday nights, "Kup's Place". At the beginning of each show, Kup would greet his viewers with "Welcome to the lively art of conversation."

We can still recall a typical Bears game radio refrain, that went something like this:

Brickhouse:

"Wait a minute, watch out now, Title's over center. He hands off to Gifford. He's tackled by Atkins, Leggett, George, Fortunato, Petitbon, and others."

Kupcinet:

"Dat's right Jack."

We are puzzled as to how we never managed to speak with the Bears TV announcers, Harold "Red" Grange, the "Galloping Ghost" or "Wheaton Iceman", and George Connor, Bears linebacker. Both gentlemen are in the Pro Football Hall of Fame. How could we have allowed this to happen? Oh, well!

While not a formal coach, Hall of Fame Quarterback, Sid Luckman, also attended most Saturday practices and then the games. Paddy Driscoll, Hall of Fame member, would watch each game on the sideline near the bench. Paddy was considered the best drop kicker in the early days of football. The defensive line was coached by Joe Stydahar, also a Hall of Fame member.

On game days, Ed McCaskey, son-in-law of Coach Halas and husband of the Coach's daughter, Virginia, would enter the clubhouse around 12:30 and watch the game from the sideline.

Brent Musburger was often in the clubhouse interviewing players as a sportswriter for the "Chicago American" newspaper. Brent went on to become a featured sports announcer for CBS Sports and is credited with coining the phrase "March Madness" to describe the NCAA Men's Basketball Tournament. He then joined ESPN and ABC Sports.

The Bears had great players during our tenure:

Doug Atkins (Pro Football Hall of Fame) was the largest of the Bears. His locker was the first one on the right when coming into the clubhouse from the shower and training area. The only radio in the clubhouse was above Doug's locker and he controlled what was being played. In the days before FM radio, there was a country western station and two rock and roll stations, WLS and WCFL. Doug loved the country and western music. When Doug left the clubhouse for the field, we immediately changed from country western to rock. He was furious each time he returned to learn that we had changed the station.

Doug was a fantastic defensive end. On the field he was unstoppable, but once he left the field, he would lackadaisically take the last chair away from the clubhouse and chat with the fans sitting along the low left field wall. When the Bears offense failed, he would express disgust and then slowly walk back onto the field only to wreak havoc on the other team's offense. We considered Doug the most dominant defensive player.

Doug was 6'8" tall and in college was a champion high jumper. Our fondest memory of Doug was against the Rams when he vaulted over the offensive lineman, fell to the ground, and from a laying position grabbed the ankles of Roman Gabriel and bent him backwards until Roman fell. A successful sack of a quarterback who was 6'5" tall!

The Bears football shoes had two sets of spikes, nylon and rubber. The nylon spikes had a hexagonal base and could be put on or replaced using a gear wrench or a power drill with the proper fitting. The rubber cleats were smooth and round and were put on or removed with pliers. Coach Halas preferred the rubber cleats and, thus, they were used most often.

One particular game (perhaps the game when Gale Sayers scored 6 touchdowns), the field was quite soggy and wet. Coach Halas decided to send the entire team out to the pregame warmup wearing the rubber spikes. Their warmup lasted roughly from 12:15 to 12:40 and the games began at 1:05. The players complained that the rubber spikes did not provide enough traction, thus Coach Halas came into the clubhouse stating that each player's spikes had to be changed to nylon. We had 25 minutes to change 40 players' spikes. The rubber spikes were wet and muddy, which made it almost impossible to remove them as the pliers kept slipping. The players were upset that their spikes were not being finished first. Doug stood up and said "Leave the twins alone. The twins have never let us down. Let them do their job." We were so grateful to him and got the job done.

Almost all players and coaches referred to us as "Twin". Only a few of the players knew our first names.

Doug was also humorously famous for leaving the strongest odor after defecating in the washroom facilities. In 1966, Doug was dethroned by Frank Cornish, a large defensive tackle drafted out of Grambling State University. We yelled out. "Move over Atkins, there is a new champion!"

Mike Ditka, a member of the Pro Football Hall of Fame, was a phenomenal athlete and the most intense of any player during the game. In our first game, Carl tried to place a jacket on his shoulders. Feeling someone coming from behind, Mike just missed Carl with a mean elbow. It was a reflex action that was not meant to be personal. Thereafter, Carl only approached him if asked.

Mike would often complain on the sidelines to Coach Halas that he was not being used properly and that the play calling was not appropriate. He wanted the ball thrown to him more often. After one such argument during a sideline timeout, Rudy Bukich threw the ball Mike's way, but it was intercepted. Mike was furious! Carl stayed as far away from Mike as possible after that play.

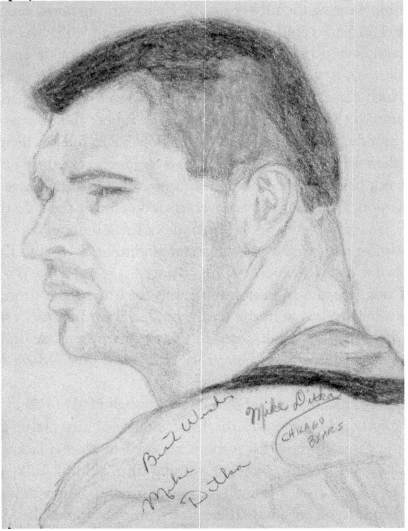

Mike Ditka Drawing

Mike knew that we ran in high school and often inquired as to how we were doing. At the University of Pittsburgh, one of Mike's classmates was Jerry Richey who was a great runner. Mike would often discuss him with us.

Bill George was also a favorite player of ours. He took an interest in us ever since our encounter on our first day of work. He became a member of the Pro Football Hall of Fame. Perhaps his greatest game was when the Bears shutout the 49ers in that shotgun game in 1961. Bill died in a car accident in September 1982. Tony was with his wife, Anne in Kentucky, but Carl attended the funeral. Afterwards he was invited to lunch by Bill and Marilyn Bishop. Also, at the lunch table were George Blanda and Fred Biletnikoff, star quarterback and wide receiver, respectively, for the Oakland Raiders.

Carl talked with Fred about the use of "Stickum", a compound used by receivers to assist them in catching a slick ball. Carl, using a wooden tongue depressor, applied an amount to the stockings of each skilled position upon their request. The players would touch their fingers to their stockings to apply the proper amount. John Madden, former coach of the Oakland Raiders and prominent NFL television announcer, brought Stickum and the use of it by Biletnikoff into the living rooms of every viewer.

We tried it often. It made our fingers slicker and was a hindrance, especially in cold weather. The NFL outlawed the use of Stickum in 1981.

Johnny Morris was a fantastic flanker back, leading the league with a record number of receptions in 1964 with 93, for 1200 yards. This held up as the NFL record until 1984! Mike Ditka was second with 75 receptions for 897 yards. This was then a record for tight ends!

From our perspective, most of Johnny's receptions were not the result of head or body fakes but from running to a certain point where he would merely turn around and catch the ball that had already been thrown to that spot mostly by Billy Wade and also by Rudy Bukich. Johnny began his career as a running back and once held the world record for the 50- yard dash. He helped popularize the flanker back position and remains the Bears all-time leader in receiving yards.

The professional football players made moderately high salaries but often worked during the offseason and needed extra income. Morton East High School needed a speaker for its athletic banquet and Johnny agreed to be the featured guest at no charge. After retirement, Johnny became the sports reporter for Channel 2 television. He later became sports anchor for the station and hosted the Mike Ditka show. When we started our accounting business with Tony's wife Anne, Johnny learned of our new beginning and called Carl at home congratulating him and wishing him good luck.

Tony, Johnny Morris, Carl

Joe Fortunato was a great strong side linebacker. We remember two things about Joe. Once he had a bathroom accident while playing. Carl had to run in the clubhouse with him to replace his pants which were covered with brown stains! Joe called all the defensive signals before the arrival of Dick Butkus. One game against the Baltimore Colts, he and the rest of the defense came off the field in laughter. They had pretty much figured out each play that was being called by famed quarterback, Johnny Unitas. On one play, near the Colts own 10-yard line, Johnny pulled out of his center a split second too soon. The ball spun off the top of his hand into the air with a perfect spiral. Joe caught the ball in mid-air and strolled into the end zone for a touchdown! We had never seen this before or since.

Larry Morris was a terrific outside linebacker. He was from Atlanta, Georgia and spoke with a slow, southern drawl. Larry spoke in soft tones, but wreaked havoc on the field. He was named as a linebacker on the NFL 1960s All-Decade Team.

Roosevelt "Rosey" Taylor was our most favorite player. Ever since our first meeting at Soldier Field, he took a special interest in us. Always discussing football, our schoolwork, our running, etc. In 1963 he led the NFL with 9 interceptions. He always said we brought him good luck. After an interception, he would often hesitate while attempting to run it back. Our Uncle Tom said we should tell him that he should imagine that a rope was tied around his waist and we were pulling him forward. One game shortly thereafter he returned an interception for a touchdown. Coming off the field, he came over to us and exclaimed, "tell your uncle that the rope worked!"

One Saturday during practice we asked Roosevelt Taylor to guard Carl while Tony passed. We asked Rosey to really try as we wanted to test our skills. He agreed and we completed the passes. Rosey then called Bennie McRae to participate and see if he could stop us. He too was unsuccessful. They both then called J.C. Caroline, at which time defensive coach George Allen blew his whistle stating, "that is enough embarrassing my boys".

In the summer, we wrote to Rosey and anxiously awaited his letters in return. He really and truly cared about our progress in school. We made sure that we introduced him to our parents. What a great guy!

Tony, Rosey Taylor, Carl

Mike Pyle was a star player for New Trier high school in Winnetka, a north shore suburb, and graduated from Yale University. He was the offensive captain of the Bears. When we were in high school, Morton East was part of the Suburban League with New Trier, Oak Park, Proviso East, Evanston, Niles East, Highland Park, and Waukegan. We would often talk about the Suburban League. He knew that we ran cross country and track. As a high schooler at New Trier he was the state of Illinois champion shot putter and discus thrower. When we applied to Yale for admission during our senior year of high school and our last year with the Bears, Mike was kind enough to write a personal recommendation on our behalf.

When we attended our 40-year Yale reunion in 2011, Mike was at Yale celebrating his 50th year reunion. He was in great shape, physically and mentally. At the Bears NFL Championship 50th year reunion in 2013 he had slipped quite a bit. He was using a walker and had deteriorated both physically and mentally.

His condition took a severe downturn soon thereafter. He was placed in the Silverado Memory Care Unit in Highland Park, where he died after being there for 18 months. We did our best to visit him. His swift decline brought further attention to the CTE problem in football.

Ronnie Bull had been NFL rookie of the year in 1962. He was an excellent running back, but had the misfortune of playing the same position as Gale Sayers. In our last years, Ronnie was used less and less. He would complain to Coach Halas on a frequent basis. Ronnie and Mike Ditka were the only two players that we were aware of that argued with the coach.

Bobby Joe Green was a fabulous punter. We often caught his kicks during practice. Catching his punts sure took some getting used to. After taking a few in the throat, we figured out the trajectory and became quite adept at catching the punts. The San Francisco 49ers and Los Angeles Rams were the only teams that practiced at Wrigley on Saturdays before the Sunday game. At their practice in 1963, the Ram punter, Danny Villanueva was punting to Jon Arnett and Dick Bass. Arnett and Bass were testing sunglasses and had difficulty catching the punts. Carl asked if he could try. The punt came down near the sideline and Carl, without the glasses, fell over a folding chair while making the catch. He held onto the ball. They were quite impressed. What a moment!

Carl, Bobby Joe Green, Tony

Bob Jencks and Roger LeClerc were both kickers. Jencks used a small plastic tee, while LeClerc used a large wooden tee built up with tape. Tony was responsible for maintaining the tees during the game. We preferred Jencks over LeClerc when it came to kickoffs. One game, Coach Halas called for LeClerc to kickoff. Tony pretended he could not find the wooden tee, so Jencks kicked off. The Coach did not seem to notice, and the kickoff had no consequence.

Rudy Bukich became the starting quarterback in 1965. His nickname was Rifle Rudy as he threw a fast, hard pass. We were both quite accomplished skill players, especially passing and catching. We often played in the alley behind our home. We would practice throwing the ball as fast as we could to each other, starting about 10 yards apart, gradually decreasing the distance. We often played 2 against 3 or more in the alley and were successful because the other team did not want to get their hands hurt by the ball.

Tony often warmed up Rudy before the game. On one particularly cold gameday, Rudy started firing the ball to Tony. Tony would catch it and fire it back. After a few exchanges Rudy complained that Tony's passes were hurting his hands. Tony replied, "What do you think your passes are doing to mine?"

We took a special interest in the younger Bears players, attempting to instill confidence in their play.

Larry Glueck, a rookie cornerback from Villanova, was the youngest player on the team. He did not turn twenty-two until October 5th. We had many wonderful conversations with Larry, many of which pertained to our wish that he be elevated to the starting lineup.

Eldon Schulte and Mike Rabold were members of the Bears taxi squad. Eldon was a linebacker from Central College in Iowa and Mike was an offensive guard from Indiana University. As they had very few responsibilities on Saturdays and no responsibilities on game days, both would engage us in frequent conversation.

In the summer of 1964, we wrote Eldon and received a wonderful reply. He was cut before that season started. Sometime around 2012, we reached him by telephone. We were disappointed that he had no memory of us. The lack of memory was explained in his 2016 obituary. He died following a lengthy struggle with Lewy Body Dementia.

Mike died in an auto accident in 1970 at age 33.

We had few responsibilities during half-time and often would play catch on the field. At that time, the goal posts were on the goal line. Tony would often send Carl between the goal posts (then in front of the left field bleachers) for 45 to 55 yard "bombs". The crowd would go nuts cheering us. The Bears half-time coordinator and business manager, Rudy Custer, would often be upset because we were taking attention away from the marching band.

In 1964 and 1966 particularly, the Bear's offense left much to be desired. They would often go three plays and out. The fans in the left field bleachers and the left field box seats and grandstand would often start a chant, "Put the twins in". Coach Halas would look at Tony who responded, "they saw us play".

From reading the playbook when there were no immediate duties in the clubhouse, we learned that most plays were designed to cause misdirection by the defender. We learned the names and "codes" of most of the plays. These were games before electronic communication between the quarterback and coaches. Often when the Bears offense was not successful, Billy or Rudy would come to the sidelines for discussion and instructions from Coach Halas and offensive coaches Jim Dooley, Phil Handler, Abe Gibron, Chuck Mather, and Luke Johnsos. As Tony often stood or kneeled directly next to Coach Halas, he would often chime in with a suggestion for the play such as "63 South Mo Lens Brown Right will work". Coach Halas and his assistants would look at Tony who would reply: "It will work"!

Coach Halas had one strict rule in the clubhouse. He did not allow smoking. Richie Petitbon, star safety of the team liked to smoke before the game as did Rudy Bukich, Roger LeClerc and later Jon Arnett and some other players. They would ask us if they could come into our cramped equipment room to smoke out of the Coach's sight. The room had only one door, no windows, and no ventilation. There was a bench alongside the wall to the player area that they would sit on and smoke. Their heads were just below the ceiling.

One time we came up with a plan to pull a joke on the smokers. Tony left the room, returning by kicking the door with Carl shouting "Here come the old man" (the player's nickname for Coach Halas). The players scrambled, hitting their heads on the ceiling, as if their parents or teachers caught them smoking in their youth.

In 1964, Jon Arnett, Dick Evey, Andy Livingston, and Jim Purnell joined the team with Larry Rakestraw on the taxi squad.

"Jaguar Jon" Arnett had been a star with the Los Angeles Rams and admired Carl's punt catching ability. In the December 12, 1965 game against the 49ers when Gale Sayers scored six touchdowns, Coach Halas took Gale out of the game with the ball on the 49er two-yard line, replacing Gale with Jon. Jon scored the final touchdown of the game. Gale was deprived of recording his seventh touchdown.

Gale's six touchdowns tied the record for the most touchdowns scored in one game by a single player. That record still stands today. Our memory is that Coach Halas explained that the 49er defense knew that Gale was getting the ball and feared that Gale may get hurt. Our opinion is that Coach Halas had such a value for NFL history that he did not want someone to break the record of six held by Ernie Nevers of the Chicago Cardinals. On November 28, 1929 Nevers set an NFL record scoring all 40 points in the Cardinals 40-6 victory over the Chicago Bears.

Before one game, Doug Evey, a defensive tackle from the University of Tennessee, came to the equipment room for a different pair of game socks. His reason was that the socks were a slightly different color. Finding spare equipment was often a challenge in that small room. We managed to find a new pair and gave it to him. He soon returned complaining that he did not want those either. The orange stripes did not align. We told him that the offensive lineman in front of him and no one in the crowd would notice.

Andy Livingston came to the Bears as a 19 year- old from Arizona who had left Phoenix College soon after entering. The NFL had granted him a hardship exemption allowing him to leave early. Andy is the youngest player to ever play in the NFL and the youngest to score an NFL touchdown at 20 years and 53 days of age. His first time touching the ball, Andy scored a 88 yard touchdown.

When we went to the Bears training camp with Sid Luckman, Coach Halas asked if we could retrieve balls. He took us and Andy to a separate area of the field where he had Andy practice kicking. Andy had told the Coach that he was a good kicker. Andy was terrible! We all realized the folly!

Andy knew that we ran track and we often spoke with him about it. We remember asking what events he ran. Andy replied the 220- yard dash. "How did you do?" we asked. He replied, "I hold the state record." "Was that your only event?", we asked. "No" he replied, "I also ran the 440- yard dash." "How did you do?" we asked. He replied, "I hold the state record."

We had no cause to disbelieve Andy. Afterall, this was running, not kicking!

In those days it was considered suicide to stop while running with the ball. We remember one game against the Packers when Andy ran around the end, only to be face-to-face with Ray Nitschke, the Packer's hall of fame linebacker. Andy stopped. Oh boy! We thought here comes trouble. We could not believe it when Nitschke stopped too, and Andy ran around him for a large gain.

Andy would often ask Tony to call his girlfriend(s) to arrange his date(s) after the game.

Jim Purnell was a linebacker from the University of Wisconsin. In one game he had his bell rung. Concussion protocol in the 1960s were as follows: After being revived with smelling salt, he was taken out of the game to sit on the bench. There were two team doctors on the sidelines, Dr. Fox, an orthopedic surgeon and Dr. Braun, a generalist. Dr. Braun instructed Carl to sit next to Jim on the bench and to periodically ask Jim to read the scoreboard and tell him the score of the game. When Jim could read the score correctly, Carl was to tell the coaches so that he could go back in the game.

Jim died in 2003 at age sixty-one of brain cancer. We wonder if there was any connection to that concussion.

In 1965 the Bears had one of the greatest drafts in NFL history selecting Dick Butkus, linebacker from the University of Illinois, and Gale Sayers, running back from the University of Kansas. Butkus was drafted 3rd overall and Sayers 4th. The Bears also drafted Dick Gordon, wide receiver from Michigan State; Jimmy Jones, wide receiver from Wisconsin; and Ralph Kurek, running back also from Wisconsin. Brian Piccolo joined the team as a free agent in 1965.

Dick Butkus, in our opinion, was the greatest middle linebacker of all-time.

The Bears always played a preseason game against the St. Louis Cardinals at Soldier Field. This game, "The Armed Forces Game", raised money for our country's servicemen and servicewomen. The Bears brought the clubhouse boys from their training camp in Rensselear, Indiana as a reward for their efforts. As a result, we had different game day responsibilities and worked the Cardinal sideline.

The Cardinal head coach, Wally Lemm, gathered the team around him for the pregame huddle. Paraphrasing the coach:

"The Bears have a hot shot rookie middle linebacker, Dick Butkus. Let's show him this isn't college. This is the NFL!"

The first half was dominated by the Bears defense, especially Butkus. The coach gathered the team around him for the second half huddle. Paraphrasing Coach Lemm: "I was completely wrong. Dick Butkus is the greatest middle linebacker I have ever seen."

It should be noted that the Cardinal defense included defensive linebackers Dale Meinert who made the Pro Bowl team in 1963, 1965, and 1967; and Bill Roman who made the Pro Bowl team in 1962 and 1964.

We noticed that Dick often stuck his fingers in the face mask of an opponent when pushing himself up off the ground after a completed play. He seemed to have the perfectly timed knack of piling on a tackle without being penalized for a late hit. He delivered the maximum punishment to every opponent!

His knowledge of the game was unchallenged. He called all the defensive formations for all players: the lineman, himself and other linebackers, and the defensive backfield. We often sat in on the Saturday defensive meetings held in the players area of the clubhouse. George Allen, the head defensive coach, would show film of the next day's opponent's previous game(s). He would indicate keys the players were giving as to what was going to happen. All defensive players were in attendance.

To us it was like being in school. George Allen would often stop the film, ask what key was give and why it would predict the upcoming play. Dick would always answer. George would get tired of Dick always providing the answer and would ask other players. They would each reply when individually and directly asked: "Dick knows, he'll let us know tomorrow." It seemed like we were sitting in our high school English class!

We remember a game when Dick met Jim Brown (most likely the greatest running back of all-time) head on. Dick bent Jim Brown backwards. When opposing teams would kickoff short and Dick was on the field, they soon learned it was not a good idea. Dick would get the ball and often return it 30 yards or so as no one could tackle him.

We also remember when Dick broke his wrist. A cast was put on his wrist and foam rubber padding wrapped around the cast. Dick was ready for action! He used the cast like a hammer!

Dick was one of the players most interested in how we were doing in school when we visited the team while on vacation from college.

Gale Sayers was a very soft-spoken person. Gale's ability to stop and change directions on a dime was unchallenged. Additionally, he had running power that was underappreciated because of his speed. He also refused to run out of bounds. He was always advancing the ball as far as he could.

Our fondest memory of Gale is his six- touchdown game against the 49ers. In that game Gale scored on an 80 yard pass play, ran for a 21 yard touchdown, ran for a 7 yard score, followed with a 50 yard rushing touchdown, then a I yard run for a score, and lastly a 85 yard punt return. The game was played on a very sloppy field. It is possible that this is the game when were under pressure to change the players spikes in the short time between warmup and the game start.

While Tony was leisurely watching exciting events, Carl was busy tending to player needs. This day was quite challenging. The mud would cake on the shoes of all the players. Carl's main job this game was to clean the players spikes when they came off the field. Protocol was to clean the shoes of the skilled positions first, starting with the quarterback, then the running backs, then the ends, and, if time permitted, the lineman. As the players sat on the bench extending their legs, Carl would go down the line scrapping all the shoes he could.

One player always motioned Carl to not clean his spikes but to service the next player. That player was Gale Sayers. Gale scored 6 touchdowns with mud caked at the bottom of his shoes. Our father sat next to his first wife, Linda during this game. This was one of only two games our father attended. The first being the 1963 championship game.

Tony was usually the first person to shake Gale's hand when he left the field after scoring. Given our size, Tony most likely greeting Gale with a "low five". The night of each game we watched the highlights on the TV sport segments to see if we could see ourselves. Gale's brilliance provided many opportunities. "Are we really that bowlegged?"

We were not knowledgeable about Gale's close relationship with Brian Piccolo. For the most part, Gale kept to himself. He was always very polite and friendly. We were not surprised however, when Gale's and Brian's close relationship was made into a movie "Brian's Song", based on a book written by Gale and Al Silverman titled "I Am Third".

Because we had remembered Gale as being extremely quiet, and Brian's illness took place after we stopped working for the Bears to go to college, Billy Dee Williams portrayal of the "Kansas Comet" did not resonate with us.

However, James Caan gave an accurate portrayal of Brian. Brian spoke with a slow, southern drawl and had a great sense of humor. His locker was next to Gale's which was typically crowded with reporters getting postgame interviews. On the side edge of his locker, Brian affixed a strip of tape. Much like parents who kept a record of their children's' height with a marker on the wall, Brian so to kept track of his yardage on the tape. He would playfully point out the tape to the reporters to highlight his accomplishments

Dick Gordon was a fabulous wide receiver who we felt was underutilized during our years with Bears. In 1965 he had 13 receptions and 15 receptions in 1966. In 1970 he led the NFL with 71 receptions for 1,026 yards. The next summer before going to graduate school, Tony drove to Rensselaer one afternoon to see the Bears practice. There was much discussion in the media regarding Dick's intent to hold out for more money.

Tony went to Dick's room and asked how he was doing. Dick replied that physical contact practice was to begin the next day and he was informed that, if he did not participate, he would be fined. Tony asked Dick if he had been doing the nonphysical contact workouts thus far. He replied that he had not. Tony's response was that it would not be unusual for an athlete beginning training to pull a muscle. Dick knew exactly where Tony was leading and pulled a muscle. He went on to have 43 receptions in 1972.

Dick was one of the first NFL players to wear his hair in the Afro style and wear flashy clothes. In a November 12, 1969 newspaper article, Coach Jim Dooley stated, "A few of our players are more interested in their hairstyles and modeling clothes than they are in playing football." The article was headlined "Bears bench 'lackadaisical' Gordon."

We always felt that Dick was misunderstood. He was one of a very few athletes that successfully completed the difficult training regimen of Dick Woit of the Chicago Lawson YMCA. Dick Woit also helped Gale Sayers recover from his infamous knee injury suffered in 1968.

Jimmy Jones was underutilized as a receiver. We championed his cause to be more involved in the Bear's offense. He treated us with interest and respect. He was terrific!

Ralph Kurek also took special interest in us. He later became an executive with the J. Walter Thompson advertising agency in Chicago, one of Hayes Lochner's largest clients.

In 1966, Larry Rakestraw, quarterback from the University of Georgia, made the active roster. Bears draft picks included Doug Buffone, linebacker from Louisville; Charlie Brown defensive back from Syracuse; and Curtis Gentry, cornerback from the University of Maryland Eastern Shore.

Larry Rakestraw realized that we had learned much of the Bears playbook by retrieving the plays from the coaches' garbage cans and asking the players the meanings of the terminology. We had the formations, codes, and plays memorized. We recognized the success of having defenders move one way while the final offensive movement was moving the opposite way. Each Saturday before the games, we would instruct Larry (should he ever get into a game) which plays he would call and in which order and why. We would often then quiz him. "What is the first play you are going to call? What is the second? Why? The third? Why?"

On November 12, 1967, we were in college. Larry got his first start against the New York Giants. New Haven television carried primarily the New York City stations. We were lucky enough to watch the game. Larry threw three touchdown passes and ran for two additional touchdowns. We were ecstatic as Larry was calling the plays we suggested. Unfortunately, Larry would break his leg and retired after the 1968 season.

One day most likely around 2008, we told Yosh Kawano this story. Yosh said it would be great to contact him. We tracked down his number and called. Larry confirmed that he indeed used the plays we had gone over with him in 1966, the year before his start. Wow!

Doug Buffone continued the Bears tradition of great linebackers: Bill George, Larry Morris, Joe Fortunato, and Dick Butkus. Our most vivid memory of Doug is a hit he put on Paul Horning. Horning's storied NFL career was soon to come to an end. Doug would always greet us with warmth and sincerity when we met throughout the years. He later became a beloved anchor on the Score AM670 sport talk radio station.

We took an instant liking to Charlie Brown and Curtis Gentry. They both were interested in us twins. The friendliness of

Charlie and Curtis helped ease the sting of their replacing Larry Glueck on the Bears roster.

After a Cubs game in 1980 or so, Carl was driving home using Lake Shore Drive. The driver in the car alongside continuously honked his horn to get Carl's attention. It was Charlie Brown! We had not seen Charlie since leaving the Bears for college after the 1966 season!

It was hard to believe that Charlie had remembered! What excitement. In later years, we asked Charlie how he could remember us. After all, we had only been with him for a total of 14 days in 1966. Charlie remarked, "You were part of the team!"

Curtis Gentry became a college coach and an educator. Carl reconnected with him when Carl's wife received an Associate's Nursing Assistant Degree from the College of Lake County and at benefits supporting one of our clients. Although "Pro Football-Reference.com" lists Curtis as being 78 years old, he is really 82. Curtis subtracted four years from his true age before the NFL draft as he felt that he would be bypassed as a 29 years old defensive back from an all-black college.

In our four years with the Bears we never witnessed any forms of prejudice or racism among the players and coaches. Everyone seemed united in the goal of winning football games.

One of Tony's prize possessions is a picture he drew of Coach Halas with his arm on the shoulder of Sid Luckman. Both Coach Halas and Sid were kind enough to autograph the drawing. Sid Luckman is also in the Pro Football Hall of Fame. During his twelve years (1939-1950) with the Bears, he led them to four championships. While not a formal coach, Sid was often in attendance on the weekends we worked. On Saturday's we would play catch with him. We felt bad for this old man. He could barely grasp the football. Maybe about ten years ago, it dawned on us that he was only 47-50 years old during our years with the Bears. "Ouch!"

George Halas and Sid Luckman drawing

The evening of September 24, 2019, R. D. Rosen, the author of "TOUGH LUCK: Sid Luckman, Murder Inc. and the Modern NFL" spoke at the Winnetka, Illinois Book Stall. He spoke of growing up in Highland Park, Illinois near the Luckman home. The original concept of Mr. Rosen's book was a fictionalized account of him playing catch with Sid on the street. This led to another Ruzicka twin moment: Perhaps we were truly the last people to play catch with this great Hall of Famer. Fact, not fiction!

Mr. Luckman became the president of Cel-U-Craft in Chicago. One day as was our custom, we went to his office unannounced. He gladly met with us and told us he was soon leaving for an afternoon visit to the Chicago Bears training camp at St. Josephs College in Rensselaer, Indiana. He asked if we would like to go with him! We called our mother and she said it was ok. We went to see the Bears with Sid, riding in his limousine, complete with a small television set. Driven by his chauffer, we watched the Cubs game as we road to training camp!

One summer our family drove to Rensselaer. We were thrilled to introduce the players and coaches to our parents. Our father conversed with Coach Halas in their native Czech language. It was a terrific experience.

On November 18, 1979, we attended the 1963 World Champion Chicago Bears Reunion Dinner. In attendance were Roosevelt Taylor, Bobby Jencks. Larry Morris, Johnny Morris, Bob Kilcullen, Roger Leclerc, Billy Wade, John Johnson, Joe Fortunato, Larry Glueck, Doug Atkins, Angelo Coia, Jim Cadile, Ed O'Bradovich, Ronnie Bull, Joe Marconi, Mike Pyle, Bobby Joe Green, Rick Casares, Dave Whitsell, and Ted Karras.

Also attending was Audrey Galimore, widow of Willie Galimore who had died with John Farrington in a car crash on July 27, 1964 in Rensselaer, Indiana, not far from the Bears training camp. Mrs. Galimore was excited to meet us and told us we were Willie's favorites. Just like our Uncles with Bronko Nagurski, Willie let us tackle him on one Saturday. Unlike Bronko, Willie was not injured.

At that dinner, we acquired "Halas By Halas", the Autobiography of George Halas, which was released that year. Reading the book provided insight as to why Coach Halas welcomed us to the Bears in 1963. We learned of Coach Halas' Bohemian heritage. As a boy he grew up in the Pilsen neighborhood of Chicago at 18th Place and Wood. He fondly remembered playing softball in the street using manhole covers and sewer grill covers as bases. He stated that as often as possible he would go to the entrance to Cubs' Park, then at Polk and Wood and wait for his heroes to enter. After graduating from high school, his mother insisted that he work before going to college. He worked at Western Electric Company in Cicero as did his two best friends and his future wife. Later, he developed real estate in a section of Cicero.

After firing Neill Armstrong as head coach in 1981, Coach Halas began his search for the replacement. Among the candidates were George Allen and Mike Ditka. Mike was a fierce competitor and one of only a small number of players that had the courage to stand up to Coach Halas. We phoned Coach Halas at his home (his number was also listed in the phone book!) and told him "Mike was one of the few players to stand up to you. He is the kind of person you want to coach the Bears."

In 1973, Mike was a coach for the Dallas Cowboys. On Sunday, September 16 they played in Chicago against the Bears. On Saturday night, Carl was downtown and ran into Mike outside of the Executive House hotel. What Carl thought would be a short conversation turned into a discussion lasting an hour or so. Mike relayed how much he missed the Bears and how he wanted to be remembered as a Bear. He longed to reconnect with Coach Halas.

Carl told him how we wrote George Halas in 1962 asking him if we could be clubhouse boys. Carl encouraged Mike to write a similar letter. In Coach Ditka's Wikipedia page there is a statement that Ditka sent a letter to Coach Halas, informing Mr. Halas that he would like to come back to Chicago and be head coach.

For us, "the Coach" was always Coach Halas, "Mike" was Mike.

About once a year, we visited Coach Halas at his office located at 55 East Jackson Boulevard. We would give each other updates, speaking about our jobs, health, and family. We seldom talked about the Bears. Coach Halas died on October 31, 1983. We went to the funeral mass at St. Ita Roman Catholic church on Chicago's North Side. In the pew behind us sat Mayor Bilandic and his wife Heather.

In January of 2008, we and our spouses went to the wake for Jim Dooley, former assistant coach and, later, head coach of the Bears. We informed his family that Jim was always kind to us. He was very mild mannered and soft spoken. Afterwards we dined at astronaut Jim Lovell's restaurant. We were privileged to meet the Captain. In 1968, Astronaut Lovell commanded Apollo 8, becoming one of the first three humans to orbit the moon.

At the Chicago parade in 1969 celebrating the astronauts from the Apollo 11 moon landing, Tony had been whisked away by security when he attempted to approach the car of Astronauts Neil Armstrong, Buzz Aldrin, and Mike Collins. Things can't always go our way! Maybe he needed Carl to be at his side!

Chip Beck, pro golfer, was also dining at the restaurant. As we had become avid golfers, this was a coup.

Carl at Wrigley old
clubhouse door

Tony at Wrigley old
clubhouse door

May 2013 we were invited by one of our long-time clients, the Illinois Humanities Council, to participate in their program, discussing neighborhoods and their importance to society. We were interviewed by David Haugh of the Chicago Tribune. Later in August we were contacted by David who wished to write an article about us as the Tribune was honoring the Bears 1963 NFL championship team. We met at "Beef and Brandy" restaurant in downtown Chicago. The wonderful article made the front page of the September 1, 2013 sports page, "Along for championship ride, twins had a ball, boy."

Bears 50th year reunion 1963 championship

We had previously provided the Bears office in Lake Forest with copies of the letters we had received form Coach Halas. The Bears front office cordially invited us to attend the 50th reunion of the 1963 Bears Championship team. The event was held at the Chicago Hilton Hotel Ballroom on September 14, 2013. As we drove to the event along with our wives, we cautioned each other not to expect too much. Perhaps the Bears were just being polite, and we would probably not be part of any festivities.

As we entered the Ballroom, we were immediately met by Larry Glueck, the first-year reserve defensive back on the 1963 team. As stated, we had often championed his cause to become a starter. Larry exclaimed to his family "it's the twins. They were instrumental to our team". His grandsons, Kevin and John, asked for our autographs! We were thrilled! Larry had remembered!

We were honored that Larry's thoughts were mirrored by so many of the players in attendance, most noticeably Roosevelt Taylor and his wife, Claudia.

Throughout the evening we engaged separately with the players. What fun!

We were interviewed and filmed for an episode of "Inside the Bears". The interview was pretty much free form of us relaying our experiences. We relayed our conversation with Coach Halas about hiring Mike Ditka. Evidently, our memory had merit as this was a featured part of the final production for television. The show aired on 1/17/2014 with the title "Halas Twin Ball Boys". It can be found on the following website: **www.chicagobears.com/video/inside-the-bears**.

When the photographer announced that a team picture was to be taken and invited all players in attendance to the stage, the players insisted that we join them. It was reminiscent of the chant we heard 50 years earlier: "Put the twins in!"

Our memories had not played tricks on us by enhancing our past experiences. To quote Ronnie Bull, halfback interviewed in the same "Inside the Bear" episode, "They were part of the group on Sundays"!

The scene in the movie "The Natural" where batboy Bobby Savoy picks out the winning bat, the "Savoy Special", used for Roy Hobbs walk off home run, resonates with our Bears memories. We had played a part in the Bears' success!

Were we really 64 years old, or were we high school seniors getting ready for our next game at Wrigley?

Virginia McCaskey, daughter of Coach Halas and current principal owner of the team, attended the dinner. At the time she was 90 years old. She called Tony to her table and told him "I always wondered who was holding the ball next to dad. It was you!"

The 1963 Bears roster had 40 players. At the reunion, the players ages ranged from around 70 to 80 years old. Sadly, 16 players were deceased, and of the remaining 24, at least half had some form of dementia. To reduce the incidences of concussions, Mike Ditka and we believe that a counterintuitive approach is needed, a return to the leather helmet. The modern helmets are being used as weapons. Players use their heads to block and tackle. We believe they would be far less willing to do so with only a leather helmet as protection.

Our clubhouse jobs resulted in other great experiences:

In one game, Tony remembers Fran Tarkenton of the Minnesota Vikings throwing a pass. It was coming straight to Tony on the sidelines and his first reaction was to try to catch the ball. Fortunately, in a split second he decided it was not a good idea. It was an excellent decision as Paul Flatley came flying through the air, caught the ball, and landed with his feet inbounds.

We learned to get out of the way when the Bears ran an end sweep. Just like the polo ponies unable to stop at the boards, the players would continue well past the out of bounds line.

All-time great quarterback and Heisman Trophy winner at the University of Michigan in 1940, Tom Harmon was the game broadcaster for the Detroit Lions. At one Saturday practice, his son, Mark, was observing and asked us to play catch. Mark is two years our junior.

We imagine that as seasoned veterans, with a wad of chewing gum in our cheeks, we took a spit, and said, "Sure, kid!" In truth, we were merely happy to have another playmate. Mark later became quite the actor and currently stars in the TV series "NCIS".

We also played catch with Coach Halas' grandson, Pat McCaskey. Pat later became vice president of the Chicago Bears.

When we were in college, we would often assist in the locker room and sidelines for the College All-Star game. The game was played at Soldier Field and pitted the previous year NFL champion team against a team of senior college All-Stars that would soon join their respective teams in the NFL. The game was played from 1934 to 1976. Archie Manning was at one of the games. We are the same age. We can proudly claim to Peyton and Eli that we also played catch with their father.

With respect to "never overlooking the obvious", this also applies to getting autographs in our teen age years. Ron Zera was head of the visitor's clubhouse at Wrigley Field for both the football and baseball seasons. We never asked him to secure autographs for us. We guess we had outgrown the excitement.

On one Saturday practice, we did get the signatures of Ram's coach Harland Svare, cornerback Lindon Crow, and Roosevelt Grier, a member of the original Ram "Fearsome Foursome". Quoting Wikipedia, "After Grier's professional sports career, he worked as a bodyguard for Senator Robert Kennedy when Senator Kennedy was shot. Although unable to prevent the assassination, Grier took control of the gun and subdued the shooter Sirhan Sirhan".

Although we probably thought being a batboy for the Cubs was not feasible because of school, we never thought of asking Yosh Kawano for the job. He later told us he would have hired us immediately.

Following the Chicago Bears also had a positive effect for the Glencoe Golf Club. The restaurant of the club is on Cook County Forest Preserve property. As such it is subject to the Forest Preserve laws and regulations. One of those regulations banned the sale of alcohol on Forest Preserve property. In 2002,

Soldier Field was undergoing renovation. The Bears played at the University of Illinois Memorial Football stadium in Champaign-Urbana. The local ordinance did not allow the sale of alcohol on Sundays. As Bears games are played on Sundays, this caused a potential severe decline in gameday revenue.

Both the Champaign and Urbana City Councils amended their liquor laws to allow the sale of alcohol on Sundays. Tony was aware of this and persuaded Cook County to amend its liquor law to permit the sale of liquor on Cook County Forest Preserve property used as a golf club.

We chose never to consume alcohol. We often told our friends and acquaintance that "we didn't want to stunt our growth."

OUR PATH TAKES A TURN

ALTHOUGH IT IS HARD TO believe given our size of 5'5" and all of 110 pounds, we had become skilled football players. Our many practices on the street on 22nd Place, in our alley, and at the field at 19th and Lombard Ave waiting for Bill Bishop paid off! Being twins, we always had a practice partner to hone our skills. Perhaps because of our body type, short compact muscles, and the knowledge of how to use leverage, we also excelled in tackle football. This we all played without any type of equipment. It seems amazing that none of us boys ever got hurt, let alone had a serious head injury or a broken bone. Perhaps it was because of the lack of equipment rather than the use of equipment. We played tackle football, not block and ram football!

We were all set to try out for our Morton East football team when we got the letter from Coach Halas informing us that we would be clubhouse boys in 1963. As the school football games were played on Saturday mornings extending to the afternoon, we knew that we would have to change our plans. The head varsity coach, Bill Vohaska, called our Mom, asking her to convince us to play football.

"Are you sure you are calling the right number? Are you talking about my little twins?", she asked. Mr. Vohaska responded, "Mrs. Ruzicka, have you ever seen them play? You have to help change their minds." Our Mom told him that we had our heart set on being clubhouse boys for the Bears and that she felt it was a once in a lifetime opportunity that should not be passed up.

Our transistor radios were set at full volume while we sang "I Get A Round" by the Beach Boys and "Under the Boardwalk" by the Drifters.

Instead of playing football, we tried out for the indoor track team. Our brother Tom had run indoor track at Morton, so we figured we would do the same. One day, all the boys had to run the feared mile. Carl covered the distance in 5 minutes and 21 seconds, with Tony not far behind! Thinking that we were going to be sprinters, instead the coach (also Bill Vohaska) had a different idea. Carl was to run the mile and Tony the half mile. Thus, began our careers as distance runners.

The walking and riding to and from the homes of Bill Bishop, Chico Maki and others seemed to have paid off. So too did our Saturday walks to the Berwyn and Olympic theaters where we would watch the Saturday matinee after paying a 10 cent or 25 cent admission. In fact, all of us four children pretty much walked everywhere. Our 7th and 8th grade classes were held at Goodwin School on 26th Street and Austin Boulevard, about a mile from our home. The mother of one of the girls across the street called our Mom asking if she would be willing to split cab fare as we would all ride to school. Our Mom said we were going to walk and that was that!

One day that we never walked, but instead were picked up and dropped off by bus, was on Sunday mornings when we would go to Cicero Bible School. Our parents stayed home. The church was on the corner of 22nd Place and Laramie Ave., only 3 blocks away! When being dropped off, the bus driver Mr. Newter, began beeping his horn as we turned onto 55th Ave approaching 22nd Place. This seemed curious. He never so much as beeped the horn at all when dropping off the other children. Later, as adults, we would have a good laugh realizing that Mr. Newter was giving our parents fair warning to end their Sunday morning escapades!

In addition to walking to the Saturday matinees at the Olympic and Berwyn theaters, we also went to the Villas theater on the southwest corner of Central and Cermak Avenues. The theater was hurting financially, so it started showing some racier movies. We remember a 1964 movie, "Lana, Queen of the Jungle". As our parents are both deceased, we can state that we all waited in anxious anticipation for Lana to swim the backstroke!

We watched with amazement as the Beatles appeared on the "Ed Sullivan Show", singing "All My Loving", "She Loves You", I Saw Her Standing There", and" I Want to Hold Your Hand". Tony is righthanded so he became John Lennon. Carl is lefthanded so he was Paul McCartney. Our parents appreciated The Beatles talent. Our Mom often sang along to the tunes.

At first, we both were not enamored with practice. It hurt too much. We had gym class the last hour at school. Instead of going to gym, we would take the bus to Morton West High School and run on its indoor track, arriving earlier than the coaches and other boys. We would hurry up with a makeshift workout, shower, and hope to leave before Coach Vohaska arrived. A few times we miscalculated and had to exert ourselves with a legitimate workout. Our times barely improved. The same was true when we moved outdoors for the spring season.

Tony, Bob Habes, Carl High School

The two best distance runners, junior Bob Habes, and sophomore, Carl Togni were more serious in their approach. Realizing our potential, they encouraged us to go out in the fall for cross country. They told the cross-country coach, Don Hudgens, that we would help the team. The meets were held mostly on weekdays, with just a few Saturday events so it would not interfere with the Bears job.

Coach Hudgens is a wonderful, moral man! He asked us to work out hard in the summer and report for practice come September. We followed his instructions, except for the hard work out part. The first workout had us runners leaving at different intervals. When it was our turn, we then tried to catch up and pass as many runners as possible. We had never experienced such a hurting side ache. More than likely the Coach was not fooled.

Carl, Tony High School

Tony, Carl, Coach Don Hudgens

Bob Habes, now a senior, had his own car, an old Renault Dauphine. He was also dating a beautiful young woman who was also in the senior class. Bob said that if we worked out hard with him and Carl Togni, he would drive us home. Being driven in the car, along with a good-looking older woman, seemed like a great proposition. We then began to train seriously.

In the summer between our sophomore and junior years, Coach Hudgens came up with the idea of the "1000 Mile Club". We runners were to run 1000 miles during the summer. We had shirts made, kept track of our miles in a little calendar book, and had so much fun. Members were Carl Togni, Keith Grauman, Alex Augustine, Bob Nardi, Gary Jowers, Mike Shields, and us twins. We began to realize the beauty of each workout and learned there is a methodology to improvement.

Bob Nardi and Gary Jowers were huge basketball fans. The Bulls first season was 1966-1967. We suggested that they go down to the International Amphitheater and see if they could become clubhouse boys. Success! For that year Morton East High School was represented in the locker rooms of both the Bears and Bulls.

We figured that the Bulls would not be good when Gary told us he could beat a few of them "one on one." Gary had a physical likeness to the Bulls first coach, Johnny "Red" Kerr. Watching the first game on television, with a close shot of the huddle, Coach Kerr and Gary were in the exact same position, arms folded with a look of disgust on their faces. We laughed ourselves silly!

We were familiar with mediocre basketball. In the summer of 1962, the 1st Annual Chicago's American City- Wide Basketball Clinic, sponsored by the Chicago Zephyrs, was held at the Cicero Stadium. Zephyrs autographs include coach Jack McMahon and player Ralph Wells. In 1963 the Zephyrs moved to Baltimore and became the Baltimore Bullets. The team is now the Washington Wizards.

Coach Hudgens had been a star basketball player at Wheaton College. His primary job was head varsity basketball coach. He also taught Botany. Even though coaching cross country was his tertiary job, he studied the science of running. He picked the brain of Joe Newton, legendary coach of the York High School's

Long Green Line, and Dick McCallister, coach of Proviso West High School. Mr. Hudgens read books on the art of training written by Arthur Lydiard, famed New Zealand track coach, who sent Murray Halberg, Peter Snell, and others to Olympic stardom. Peter Snell at one time held the World Record in both the half mile and one- mile runs. "The Track & Field News" published Snell's times during his high school years and we used this as a comparison to our improvement. As adults, we were honored to meet both Arthur and Peter.

The training was a combination of base training (the aerobic phase) and interval training (the anaerobic phase). We thrived on these workouts, which stand up as harder workouts than most high school runners do today. Thanks to these workouts, the tutelage of Coach Hudgens, and the joy of our teammates, we had successful high school running careers.

Our parents came to almost every home meet, our Dad in his suit and our Mom in a house dress. Our teammates loved their vocal support. Gary Jowers could not break the 5 minute mile barrier. Our father had "Strive For Five Gary Jowers" cards printed and we passed them out to as many students as we could.

We immersed ourselves in the music of "the British Invasion". We teammates sang in the shower to songs of the Beatles, the Rolling Stones "(I Can't Get No) Satisfaction", "Paint it Black" and "Mother's Little Helper"), the Zombies ("She's Not There" and "Tell Her No"), the Kinks ("You Really Got Me" and "All Day and All of the Night") and the Dave Clark Five ("Glad All Over", "Any Way You Want It" and "Bits and Pieces"). We and our classmates tried to determine how many "no"s there were in "Tell her No". Through the beauty of the internet, we can state the answer is 63!

"Time is on My Side" by the Rolling Stones and "Catch Us If You Can" by the Dave Clark Five became our theme songs. On days when we felt the Coach was working us too hard, we all sang "We Gotta Get Out of This Place" by the Animals.

We also sang to "Reach Out" by the Four Tops and listened to "Baby Love" by the Supremes. Mowtown had found its groove.

While studying at our kitchen table, we would rise from our chairs, and with our Mom, march around the table to Frankie Valli and the Four Seasons singing "Opus 17"!

During this time, we formed a track club to perform in summer and off- season competitions. The club was the brainchild of Carl Togni. It was called the "CTA" track club. We all had t-shirts made, blue with the letters CTA emblazoned in red across the chest. Many people thought that the letters stood for the Cicero Track Club or Chicago Transit Authority, the initial name of the famed rock group "Chicago". In truth the letters stood for the "Carl Togni Amphibians"! We recruited Ken Ward and Dave Chancey from competing Proviso East to join in the club. Ken Ward became Illinois outdoor mile champion. Our father had CTA membership cards printed for us members.

Other runners at that time were Rick Wohlhuter from St. Charles, who was a medalist in the 1976 Olympic 800 meters, Lee Labadie from Maine West High School, and Ken Popejoy from Glenbard West. Lee and Ken later became the first two milers in the Big Ten history to break 4:00 in the mile run.

We befriended many of our competitors from the other schools. We had a friendly competition as to who could "temporarily" steal the other team's equipment. Gradually we graduated from a stopwatch or measuring tape to other equipment. Once an opponent bragged that they had stolen a ball used for the shot put. Another competitor bragged about stealing a pole used in the pole vault competition. Not to be outdone, we informed them that we had stolen the entire equipment locker of an opponent. We placed the locker in the aisle of the opponent's team bus, which we also had stolen!

Coach Hudgens helped run a Christian basketball camp in Connecticut. Realizing that us runners had newfound dedication, he asked our parents if we could attend the camp. We would run instead of practicing basketball. Our parents gave permission. Along with Carl Togni, Keith Grauman, Bob Nardi and Gary Jowers, we all piled into the Coach's car and we made the trip east to the camp.

As we approached the East Coast, we were able to pick up New York's major rock and roll station "WABC" on the car radio. We listened to Cousin Brucie spin the hits. The show seemed similar to the Chicago's WLS radio show. We first realized the existence of syndicated formats. We sang along to "A Hard Day's Night" by the Beatles. Bob Nardi and Gary Jowers did their best impression of Sonny and Cher singing "I Got You Babe"!

What a wonderful time. Even though we all worked out twice a day, our days were filled with laughter and amusement. Two camp participants were Mel Reddick, who went on to star for the University of Wisconsin in both basketball and football, and Kerry Pfund, brother of Randy Pfund, who went on to be a NBA (National Basketball Association) head coach with the L.A. Lakers and general manager of the Miami Heat.

It so happened that Coach Hudgens wife Roberta's father, Berner Lohne, was a builder in and around New Haven, Connecticut where Yale University is located. As luck would have it, he had built the home of Yale's Track Coach, Robert Giegengack, who had been head coach of the 1964 USA Olympic team that competed in Tokyo. Knowing that we had excellent grades, Coach Hudgens suggested that he drive us to Yale for an interview.

The three of us made our way to New Haven. We had the interview, which ultimately led to us applying to, and being accepted (after first being on the waiting list) by Yale University, starting in the fall of 1967, and graduating in 1971 with Bachelor of Arts degrees in Economics.

We had also learned a valuable lesson. Just as our first letter to George Halas did not bring immediate results, this held true with our applications to Yale. Sometimes we have to make additional attempts to accomplish our goals.

Our Mom and Dad each completed about a year of high school. All our aunts, uncles and cousins did not carry on their educations past high school. Our sister Barbara had excellent grades and was a great candidate for college. At that time, and certainly within our family, a woman doing so was not commonplace. Instead, she became a dental assistant for the dentist just about a block from our house.

The resultant savings of Barbara not attending college helped support the secondary education of her brothers. Tom was the pioneer. He first went to two years at Morton Junior College and the last two years at Millikin University in Decatur, Illinois. He later received a master's degree in political science from Northeastern Illinois University.

We would not have dreamt about going to Yale in a million years! We had never ever considered Yale as a choice. Our admission brought our family great pride. Our Dad reminded us of the car radio playing the Yale "Whiffenpoof Song" while he drove our Mom to the hospital for our delivery.

In 1999, at age 59, Barbara received her degree from the Aurora Colorado Community College. We all traveled to Aurora to surprise her at the cap and gown graduation ceremony! What a night! Throughout her studies, Barbara stated that, at her stage in life, the experience was the important aspect of the education, not the grades. Yet, she performed just as she did in high school.

Ah, the competitive spirit, learned playing softball in our alley, still lived within!

Our grandmother had no formal education. She emigrated to the United States when she was about 11 years old. Yet she learned parts of at least four languages. In her broken English, Grandma expressed pride that her grandsons were going to Yale "UniversiTEE".

Grandma regularly entered the weekly "Little Fooler" puzzle

(pronounced "poo zel" by her) contest in one of the Chicago newspapers. She would always get one or two wrong. One week, after getting just one incorrect answer, she had enough! She wrote the editor of the paper proclaiming:

"You are a bunch of crooks! My answer is correct, but when you see it is my entry, you change to another answer. I never want anything to do with your paper again!"

She added a P.S.:

"If you change your mind, I can be reached at 3305 W. Monroe in Bellwood, IL."

We tried our hands at the puzzle. She could not believe that we got so many wrong! "Are you sure you go to the "universiTEE"?"

We perhaps were influenced by our grandmother when writing celebrities. Grandma wrote more than one letter to Josip Broz Tito, the president of the Socialist Federal Republic of Yugoslavia, complaining of conditions in what had been Croatia, her birth country. President Tito and our grandmother were both born near Zagreb, Croatia's capital.

We are not sure if she referred to him as a "crook", such as in her letter to the newspaper editor, but she sure could be direct when the need arose. We remember that she received letters from Tito in response, but, inexplicably, the family did not save them. If any of us doubted the veracity of any of her ideas or statements, Grandma would reply, "I tell you true!"

A combination of excellent grades and good running times was part of the reason we were accepted at Yale. Another more important reason was that we fit the economic, diversity profile. Our incoming class was the first to be admitted under a program initiated by R. Inslee "Inky" Clark, Jr., the Director of Under-graduate Admissions.

As stated in Wikipedia: "For decades prestigious northeastern colleges had used "character" as a code word to limit the number of acceptances afforded to secondary school students with Jewish and working class Catholic backgrounds to colleges traditionally defined by an Episcopalian or WASP social standard. Negroes were invisible on campus. Associated with this move, Yale, followed by other prestigious colleges in the northeast section of the United States, recruited for the first time beyond the prep school orbit of New England and mid-Atlantic boarding schools, and private schools in New York, Boston, Philadelphia, Baltimore, and Washington, D.C.. This new policy is now a standard in their respective admissions practice."

While only a small percentage of our classmates were of color, Calvin Hill starred in football and track, later becoming a star running back with the Dallas Cowboys, and Kurt Schmoke played lacrosse. He later became the first African American mayor of Baltimore, Dean of Howard University School of Law, and president of the University of Baltimore.

Under Inky Clarke's leadership, for the first time, the incoming students would be equally divided between those from traditional Eastern private Prep Schools and public schools. We found out that there were many students from New Trier, our competitor in the original Suburban League, located in the north shore town of Winnetka.

We were (and remain) the only two of three students that went to Yale from Morton East. When Tony got married to his wife Anne she asked where he thought they should live. Tony told her anywhere that feeds into New Trier. They moved to Glencoe in 1975 and have lived there ever since. He served as a village trustee and later as village president.

This was in stark contrast to some of our high school experiences. When traveling to a basketball game at New Trier, some students would put belts and chains in the trunk of their cars. They may have to teach the rich kids a lesson!

After our second year, Yale began admitting women. The class entering in 1969 included 250 women, divided between first year students, and sophomores and juniors transferring from other colleges. There were no transferring seniors as two years of Yale studies would have to be completed to qualify for graduation. We are proud that our Class of 1971 was the first to graduate women. Alice Young was the first Asian woman to graduate!

Our exposure to diverse cultures while at Yale has proven to be invaluable. It has helped us to empathize with persons with different backgrounds or ideas.

There is no doubt that we were somewhat intimidated entering Yale. Our first trip to Yale for freshman year was also our first trip on an airplane. We remember that the Box Tops first hit "The Letter" which opened up with "give me a ticket on an airplane" had special meaning.

We questioned whether we would fit in with wealthy, smarter classmates. It did not help that, when reading a composite of the incoming class, we learned the average SAT scores exceeded 1500 (1600 being perfect). Our SAT scores were in the 1270 range. Another "Ouch!"

Fortunately, we soon learned that we were ahead of most in "street smarts" It also helped that we had the best sporting equipment: official Duke NFL footballs, official major league baseballs caught in the bleachers at Cubs games, and our NHL hockey sticks of Stan Mikita, Bobby Hull and Chico Maki. Helping us too, was the fact that we dominated most touch football games. After one such game, George Bermingham's girlfriend referred to us as "massive". Bliss!

We also noticed that when a few of our wealthier classmates visited our home in Cicero, our parents were not interested in their wealth, but rather in their comfort and everyday experiences. Laughter was a hallmark of such visits.

Incoming freshman were allowed only 15 meals in our residential college dining hall. Most meals were to be eaten in the Yale "Commons". We befriended the kitchen and dining room staff from our first day of arrival and they never punched our meal ticket. It was not until the campus closed in the spring of 1970 because of a student strike and "May Day" festivities that we had our first meal at the "Commons".

As a freshman, Tony worked in the dining hall of one of Yale's residential colleges, Branford. We befriended two African American kitchen workers from New Haven, Essel and Spaniel. Both grew very fond of us and we of them. Essel and Spaniel spoke extremely fast with very distinct dialects. Our classmates were amazed when we engaged them in conversation. Our classmates had no idea what they were saying, but we never missed a beat!

At our reunions, we similarly engaged the waiting staff in conversation. Once a classmate remarked that we had done this while students. We replied that those were our kind of people.

Yale had had a swimming requirement for incoming freshman. This was stopped our freshman year, but for some reason we still had to go to the pool and swim two lengths of the 50- meter pool. Tony showed up in the middle of the swim teams' practice. The swim coach was Phil Moriarty, who had served as diving coach for the USA 1960 Olympic team. In the pool, members of the team included Don Schollander and John Nelson.

Schollander won a total of five gold medals and one silver medal at the 1964 and 1968 Summer Olympics. With four gold medals, he was the most successful athlete at the 1964 Olympics. Nelson won a bronze medal in the 1964 Olympics and gold and bronze medals in 1968.

Coach Moriarty whistled everyone out of the pool, so that Tony could swim his laps. Seeing how neither of us could swim, this was going to be a challenge. Making his way slowly along the edge of the pool, Tony somehow managed one lap and got out of the water. The coach told Tony he had one more lap to go. Tony responded, "I'll come back another day to complete the next lap. You can add them up. The requirement never stated that a student has to swim two consecutive laps."

Don Schollander was a resident of Branford. He told Tony, compassionately, that he could become a good swimmer. Maybe the students at Yale were not so smart after all!

While completing our cross-country workouts, Erich Segal was often there asking us what workouts we were doing and why we were doing them. He was a professor at Yale who in 1970 wrote the bestselling book "Love Story" which later became a popular movie starring Ryan O'Neal and Ali McGraw. He also was a screenwriter for the Beatles 1968 feature "Yellow Submarine". Back home in Cicero our friends were impressed. We were more impressed that often he would drive us back to the campus, rather than us having to wait for the bus. We were able to get into the dinner meal line much earlier! Such was the practicality of our upbringing.

One night we received a telephone call around 4:00 in the morning. We feared something had happened to our parents. It was our childhood friend Gary Jowers calling from Tan San Nhut Air Force base in Vietnam. Gary was assigned to communications at the base. Gary asked, "How did the Cubs do in their last few games?"

On December 1, 1969, we and our classmates tuned our radios and listened closely to the results of the draft lottery to determine the order of call to military service in the Vietnam War. It was the first time a lottery system had been used to select men for military service since 1942.

Each day of the year (corresponding to one's birthdate) were printed on paper, placed in a capsule, and dumped into a deep glass jar. Capsules were drawn from the jar one at a time. We learned our fate with the announcement of each day, with the first date picked assigned lottery number 1, and so forth.

To determine the order of those with the same birthdate, a second lottery was performed using the 26 letters of the alphabet. The letter corresponded to the first letter of one's last name.

Our birthdate was picked number 326, and "R" was picked 19th. We appeared safe from having our lives interrupted by military service. We were extremely happy. To someone chosen with a low number (Harry Armstrong was number 2), we gave our condolences with smiles that could not be contained. We changed the lyrics to the Beatles' hit song "A Day in the Life", singing: "For some the news was rather sad, but we just have to laugh, we are 326 in the draft".

Ultimately, those with birthdates of the first 195 days picked were called to serve in some capacity.

We sang along to "Suspicious Mind" by Elvis Presley, "Brown Eyed Girl" by Van Morrison, and "Happy Together" by the Turtles.

During our four years at Yale, we often visited our sister and her family. Our freshman year, Barb, her husband Gary (Velat), and one years old daughter, Kathe, lived in Melrose, Massachusetts, a small town along route 128 in back bay Boston. Gary was a career medical officer in the Navy. He did his internship at the Chelsea Navy Base Hospital. The following year, they moved to the Groton, Connecticut, when Gary was transferred to the New London Navy base. They initially lived in Naval housing.

We would visit as often as we could, either hitching a ride or taking the New York New Haven Railroad that had a stop in New London. Each time, we would bring our laundry and a stack of books for weekend homework assignments. Barbara did our laundry, but we never opened a book. We were too busy playing with Kathe and then Barbara's second daughter, Deb. This was such a joy! Belying our education, we continued to bring our books every visit.

Reminiscent of the blunt language used by our Mom when "ordering" Ernie Banks to sign our scorecards, Barbara implored, "Why are you coming here? Is it just so I can do your laundry, feed you solid meals, and so you can spend time with the children and with Gary?" She sure knew how to make us feel guilty as we devoured another delicious meal!

On Sundays we would watch the NHL game of the week, followed by "The Smother Brothers' Comedy Hour" and "Mission Impossible". The Blackhawks rarely made appearances on the game of the week, and it was next to impossible to pick up their games on the radio.

However, one special Sunday night, the last game, of the NHL regular season, the Blackhawks were playing the Montreal Canadiens. This was the 1969-1970 season and the format for qualifying for the playoffs was changed. If teams were tied, the last spot in the playoffs would go to the team that had scored the most goals.

Montreal was the team that needed to score as many goals as possible. We went out to Gary's car parked alongside their house and were able to pick up the broadcast on his car radio. We told him that we would beep the horn to represent the score. With 9 minutes and 30 seconds to go in the third period, Montreal was down by a score of 5-2. Its only hope of qualifying for the playoffs was to score three more goals. The Canadians pulled their goalie and the Hawks scored five more goals within the 9 ½ minutes. We laughed ourselves silly, beeping the increased score every minute or so! When we went back into the house after the game, Gary could not believe it! We were all so excited! The excitement was somewhat muted the next morning when the neighbors complained about the constant, late night beeping of the horn!

The Boston Bruins won the Stanley Cup propelled by probably the worst trade in Chicago Blackhawk history. In 1967, the Hawks traded Phil Esposito (our touch football opponent), Ken

Hodge and Fed Stanfield to the Bruins for Gilles Marotte, Pit Martin, and minor league goalie Jack Norris. Boston dominated hockey for quite some time.

When visiting our sister Barbara and her family, we most often would hitch hike to Groton and then take the train back. On one trip just before final exams, a gentleman gave us a ride. Tony sat in the backseat with his books and study notes in tow. Unfortunately, he fell asleep and left the school materials in the car when departing. Once again quoting Jack Brickhouse, "Oh brother!"

We remembered that the young man that picked us up was a graduate student at Southern Connecticut State University, also in New Haven, and that his car was a red Volkswagen. While at our sister's home, Tony called the University and asked if any red Volkswagens were registered. He was provided with the numbers of three students. On his second call he struck gold and he was able to retrieve his materials in enough time to study for the final exam. Barbara could not believe our luck.

We listened to the "Days of Future Passed" album by the Moody Blues. This concept album featured "Tuesday Afternoon" and "Nights in White Satin". We went on to buy all new albums released by the group.

The 1968 Democratic Convention was held in Chicago. There were protests led by the Students Democratic Society For A Democratic Society (SDS) that turned violent. Mayor Daley uttered these famous words, "The police are not here to create disorder, they're here to preserve disorder". Bill Ayres formed the Weather Underground Organization (WHO), a radical left militant organization that proposed to overthrow American imperialism.

We gave this and other movements little credence. Upon reflection, we may have thought otherwise if the movements were not tied to the drug culture prevalent at that time. Bill Ayres became an educator in the Chicago area. We have had the pleasure to meet him at various client functions. Interesting discussions ensued.

Near the end of our sophomore year at Yale, we decided to go see the Cubs play the Mets in New York. This was the infamous 1969 season, which we thought was going to be the year of the Cubs! One game was held Friday April 25, 1969, one game on Saturday April 26, with a double header played Sunday April 27. We each had about $10.

We began the weekend trip by hitchhiking to New York. Our first ride took us roughly a quarter of the way. For the last part of the trip we were picked up by a limousine driver returning to LaGuardia airport. We rode in the back of the limousine and were dropped off directly in front of Shea Stadium!

The stadium was only about 2 1/2 miles from the airport. We bought the cheapest available tickets and entered the park for the night game.

Listening to Mets fans taunt our Cubs players, it seemed as if the Cubs had traded their shortstop, Don Kessinger and their second baseman, Glenn Beckert. Don KessinGAH (hard "G") was the new shortstop. His keystone partner at second base was Glenn BeckAHT. A new coach was Rube WalkAH! The Cubs manager was Leo DurocHAH! Vendors hawked their ice cold beahs. What fun! We were watching baseball and learning a foreign language!

We yelled to Ron Santo (who we did not know at the time), got his attention, and went down to the first row of the box seats. Ron came over and spoke with us. We told him about being from Chicago, being great Cubs fans, and our trip from Yale. Ron asked if we would like to go to the next game on Saturday. We told him we did not have tickets and little money (this was the time before credit cards). Ron told us he would leave two tickets at Will Call! What excitement. The Cubs won the game 3-1. When the game was over, we walked to LaGuardia and slept overnight in the terminal.

On Saturday morning, we got our tickets at the Will Call window, entered the ballpark, and went down near the field to thank Ron. In doing so, we asked him if he could possibly give us tickets for the next day? Ron immediately replied, "you have tickets"! We watched the Cubs beat the Mets 9 to 3. After the game we returned to our plush quarters at LaGuardia.

Sunday the Cubs beat the Mets 8 to 6 in the first game and lost to the Mets 0-3 in game 2. We now had to return to New Haven. We hitched rides. Our first ride was with Jim McAndrew's father. Jim McAndrew was the winning pitcher for the Mets that night, pitching 5 and 2/3 innings of shutout baseball, allowing only 3 hits.

Despite, the loss, the Cubs seemed to be on their way! We successfully returned to New Haven. Perhaps after buying the game one ticket, we each may have eaten one hot dog, a few candy bars, and drank a few sodas the entire time. We had a very memorable weekend!

Upon returning to school in late summer of 1969, the Cubs were in a tailspin. We decided to go to Shea Stadium to once again cheer on the Cubs against the Mets. This game was played on September 8th. Only Carl was still running at the time. Tony left for the stadium early. Carl followed after his cross country practice.

Carl arrived in the middle of the game. On his way to meet Tony, he happened to be watching from the square window right behind home plate at the very instant when Tommy Agee was called safe on a disputed tag by Randy Hundley

This play epitomized the sinking Cubs and rising Mets. It hurt us even more knowing that Tommy Agee was a former White Sox. This was the famous "Black Cat" game, with a picture published of a black cat putting a "hex" on the Cubs dugout, while Ron Santo and the Cubs bat boy waited in the on deck circle. We later became good friends with the Cubs bat boy, Jim Flood.

Agee was definitely out! Unfortunately, the Cubs ended up 8

games behind the Mets. Let's see, were there any other games of such blatant misjustice?

In May 1970, there was a large-scale civil disobedience action at Yale to protest the trial of Black Panther leader, Bobby Seale for the alleged murder of a fellow Black Panther member, turned informant. Demonstrators from around the country came for the protest.

Before the protest, we were asked to have a portion of our Yale fees diverted for use to provide food for the protestors. While not necessarily against the protest, our reply was based on our trip the previous April to New York. We explained that we had gone almost three days with little food and drink to see the Cubs play the Mets. Surely, the protests were more important. Why then could not those coming from outside New Haven to protest just have minimal food.?

Instead of feeding the protestors, we suggested giving the money to organizations such as the NAACP, organized to protect, defend, and gain civil rights by leveling the economic and educational playing field, and to promote peace and justice around the world.

The fees were used to feed the protestors.

During this period, various students from New Haven's Hill-house High School were appearing more frequently in Yale's facilities. Hillhouse was a very radical school. An increase in crime and petty theft ensued. A new policy was established that the youth could only use Yale's facilities if they were chaperoned. We befriended two inner-city boys, Kenny and Melvin.

When not in class, we would often shoot pool with them in the basement of our college, us two against them two. If they seemed to be on their way to victory, we would encourage them to "be the conservative element at Hillhouse" and tease them with other ideas foreign to their psyche. They would lose their cool, imploring us to "Cut the jive, twin!" Flustered, Kenny and Melvin would soon go cold and lose the game.

One day Carl got paid for his bursar job. When cashing his check, Carl asked to be paid with currency that included a $50 bill. We would be leaving for Chicago soon, and Carl did not want the temptation of spending his earnings. Carl took a two-minute shower. He hung his blue jeans which contained the bill on the hook outside the shower stall. Upon returning the $50 bill was missing!

Without making any accusations, Carl told the story to Kenny. Kenny reached into his wallet and counted out $50 in various bills, gave the money to Carl, and commented, "Everyone should know not to mess around with you and your brother!"

At our 45th Yale Reunion in 2016, we noted that key cards were required to enter almost every campus facility. We question whether this advancement in technology and safety should be considered progress.

Songs popular in this period took a more serious, ominous tone. These songs included "War" by Edwin Starr, "Revolution" and "Helter Skelter" by the Beatles, "White Room" by Cream, and "Woodstock" by Crosby, Stills, Nash & Young. The Beatles released their "White Album". The words "Helter Skelter" were written in blood on the wall of one of the homes of Charles Manson's murder victims.

Contrary to the norm, we anxiously awaited all songs released by the Bee Gees. Our Mom also loved their music.

We shared stories of many of our sport stories with our Yale classmates, Shad Dabaghi, Skip Rosenbloom, and Harry Armstrong, George Bermingham, and others. Skip was a transfer student from Maryland University. In discussing our respective hometowns, we discovered that Skip was from Lincolnwood, Illinois, a suburb just north of Chicago. He learned about our growing up in Cicero. Skip's father and uncle, Alex Estrin, had spent much of their early adulthood in Cicero. We immediately called home with the news and learned that Alex Estrin had been our father's best friend. What a small world!

Yale's radio station would often run contests for its listeners. We won 2nd place for entering the funniest name on campus, "Rashad Eugene Dabaghi". Another contest was to match up a current celebrity as professor of a current class offered in the curriculum. Tony's 2nd place entry was Roberto DeVicenzo teaching Math 101. DeVicenzo had recently been disqualified for signing an incorrectly added scorecard which cost him a potential victory in The Masters Golf Tournament.

On March 8, 1971, a group of us went to the New Haven Arena to watch "The Fight of the Century" on closed circuit broadcast. Muhammed Ali was fighting his first major fight after returning from a three-year suspension for refusing induction into the armed forces. He invoked his rights as a conscientious objector based on his Islam faith. He was undefeated and the heavyweight champion at the time of his suspension. Joe Frazier had claimed the title of heavyweight champion during Ali's three-year hiatus.

We created a pool to predict the winner and in what round would this occur. None of us predicted that the match would go to entire 15 rounds. Ted Swift, of the Swift & Company family, was deemed the winner as his entry was closest to the outcome. We lobbied that all money should be returned as there was not a true winner. You win some and lose some.

We note that the cost of tuition and room and board at Yale in 1971 was $3300. In today's dollars this equates to $21,307. Tuition and room and board at Yale now has a price tag of $73,900. We were able to cover our share (we split the responsibility with each of us paying 2/3 and our parents paying the remaining 1/3 for each) through earnings from our summer jobs. The loans were our responsibility and quickly paid off when we began working. Something seems wrong with the current equation!

Yale's endowment approximates $30.31 billion. That sure covers a lot of rainy days. If Yale applied approximately 1.45% of it towards undergraduate tuition and room and board, it would eliminate the need to charge its students.

We often discuss this situation with Yale classmate and Saturday morning golf partner Paul Selden. While at Yale, Paul's stepfather was the top officer at American Express Company. He had an annual salary that approximated $300,000. Our father's salary approximated $13,000 and we considered our family to be of lower middle class. Another classmate of ours, in a position similar to that of Paul's stepfather, drew recent annual salaries approximating $25 million. Using the same ratio, our father would have to be making $1, 083,333, hardly a lower middle-class income.

While at Yale, we became close friends with Al Shaw, one year our senior in school. His senior year, Al won the John L. Carey Scholarship Award given by the American Institute of Certified Public Accountants to a Yale graduate who would major in accounting in graduate school. Al attended the University of Chicago Graduate School of Business. He told us about the award and Tony applied and was fortunate to be awarded the scholarship. We both decided to follow Al to the University of Chicago Graduate School of Business to obtain our MBA degrees. Al told us we could major in accounting by taking 5 accounting classes of the 20 classes required.

In 1972, Al Shaw was in his second year at the U of C and we were in our first year. He shared Thanksgiving dinner with us at our home. Our brother Tom and his family also joined. After dinner, Al, Tom, and we went out to play some touch football on 55th Ave. We believe that Mrs. Zima was now deceased. One of us threw the football and it flew through the plastic rear window of a parked car. At ages 23, 24 and 28, we immediately started running away! What maturity!

Once we were exposed to accounting, we decided to pursue accounting careers. Carl began working for Price Waterhouse. Tony joined Arthur Young & Company where he had the good fortune of meeting his wife Anne. The Spinners' song "Could It Be I'm Falling In Love" took on a whole different meaning.

It is primarily because of Anne being chair of the Illinois CPA Society Nonprofit Committee that so much of our accounting career has been devoted to assisting the nonprofit community.

Accounting was a practical application, not theoretical like finance. Cicero was a meat and potatoes town. We were anxious to be near our parents. We had some reservations about our first leaving for Yale. Our sister and brother were already married and out of our 22nd Place residence. Our parents would be alone in their home for the first time in 30 years. Little did we suspect that our parents would thrive with our departure. When we came back home to study at the U of C, we did our best not to cramp their style.

We were also anxious to be nearer the Cubs. We grew tired of the slow turning of our transistor radio dials, trying to pick up the Cubs game. We were tired of reading box scores in the paper that were from games two days prior.

Our running careers at Yale were a disappointment. We always seemed tired and disliked coach Geigengack. He sure was different than Coach Hudgens! We caught up on our sleep on the bus when traveling to competitions. It is hard to describe the sinking feeling we felt as the bus came to a halt and the race was near.

Our freshman year, the IC4A cross country championship was held in Van Cortland Park in the Bronx area of New York City. Coach mistakenly thought the race was to begin three hours before the actual starting time. We runners had a lot of time to kill. As the other teams arrived, we sat out to find the Notre Dame team. Their members included Mike Collins, from New Trier High School and the 1965 Illinois State Cross Country champion; and Rick Wohlhuter, state half mile champion from St. Charles High School.

Coach Giegengack was furious and accused us of "consorting with the enemy". We retorted, "This isn't Vietnam Coach!"

However, on a much more positive note, we were able to form an everlasting friendship with a runner two years older, Frank Shorter, future 1972 Olympic Marathon gold medal winner in Munich, and 1976 Olympic Marathon silver medal winner in Montreal.

Our freshman year, Frank and Tony were the only members of the team with mustaches. Facial hair would become more than common place within a year or so during the "Hippy" movement

For our team picture, Coach Geigengack insisted that all his runners be clean shaven. Realizing that he needed Frank's leverage with the Coach, Tony had Frank vow not to shave his mustache. The afternoon of the picture taking, we arrived on the second bus taking us to our workout facilities near the Yale Bowl. Frank had taken the first bus. Tony's heart sunk when, upon arriving, Frank was exiting the locker facilities clean shaven. As we look passed Frank, there stood the coach, a can of shaving cream and raiser in hand!

Tony regrew the Groucho Marx like mustache and did not shave it off until a 1974 weekend trip to Geneva, Wisconsin with his fiancé, Anne. It was the first time in many years that Carl saw Tony unshaven and he was looking at his mirror image. He jokes that he was never so disappointed in his life. As we say often, there is a fine line between comedy and tragedy!

Tony and Anne's marriage took place in November of that year in Anne's hometown of Winchester, Kentucky. The Ruzicka families stayed in a row of rooms at the local Holiday Inn. Clean shaven Tony was talking with family members in the lobby. Barbara's youngest child, Dave was three years old at the time. He got very frustrated and angry that everyone was using Tony's name. "That's not Uncle Tony, that's Uncle Carl"! Just then, Carl turned the corner to join the group. Everyone pointed to him and said, "There is Uncle Carl". Never to give up and be proven wrong, Dave uttered his perfect solution: "There are two Uncle Carls"!

In the 1984 Winter Olympics, Vladimir Ruzicka starred for the silver medal winning Czechoslovakia hockey team. A lot of our friends gave us grief. "Tell him to take it easy on the USA!" Vladimir is not our relative, but our nephew Dave told everyone he was his cousin! How could that be?

We joke that during this time of long hair, mustaches, beards and the "Sexual Revolution" it seemed we always became involved with women who were conscientious objectors. More accurately, our boldness in approaching sport stars, was unfortunately the opposite when approaching (or lack thereof) young women.

Frank Shorter was already a terrific runner, but he improved substantially when he arrived for his senior (our sophomore) year. His family had moved to Taos, New Mexico from upper state New York that summer. It was then that Frank first learned the benefit of altitude training.

On Halloween night 1968, the team traveled to Princeton, New Jersey for the HYP (Harvard, Yale, Princeton) cross country championship. Halloween happens to be Frank's Birthday. After eating and lying around our rooms at the local Holiday Inn, we decided that we would go "trick or treating." Frank dismissed the idea as pure folly. Undeterred, we set out on our mission. The hotel was near Princeton's graduate school student housing. Learning our lesson from our brother Tom, Carl dressed up as Tony, and Tony dressed up as Carl.

We were a big hit! We arrived back at the hotel with two filled bags of candy. We knocked on Frank's door, unloaded the candy on his bed and proclaimed, "here you go, doubting Thomas!" Frank picked out various items, especially a few "Payday" candy bars.

The following morning Frank beat Doug Hardin of Harvard

for the first time in his career and would never lose to him again! Throughout his successful running career, Frank would eat a "Payday" candy bar before each race. We kid him that his successful career was the result of our "trick or treating" that night. Perhaps, unknowingly, he had started a journey of his own! For sure, his success in the Olympic marathons set us on a new journey.

ROAD WARRIORS

OUR RUNNING CAREERS DID NOT take off at Yale as planned. By our senior year we had both stopped running. We did not stay in touch with Frank Shorter following his graduation in 1969. We first saw Frank again when he won the 1970 U.S. National Cross-Country Championship run in Chicago's Washington Park.

As we sat home watching the 1972 Olympic marathon on television, our bodies literally shook as we watched Frank wind his way through the streets of Munich. As he got close to entering the stadium to complete his stunning win in front of thousands of fans, an imposter entered the stadium instead. The marathon announcers were Jim McKay, and our ride back to Yale's campus, Eric Segal. "That's not Frank, that's not Frank, that is an imposter, get him off the track, this happens in bush league marathons", Eric screamed into the microphone!

We could not believe that someone whom we had run so many workouts with was an Olympic champion. Yet, we were not prepared to get back into running. We were busy studying in the MBA program at the University of Chicago, working part time, and playing lots of tennis.

We played tennis at the Lakeshore Racquet Club on Fullerton Ave. We had permanent court time two nights of the week. One evening we showed up only to realize that our reserved court was being used as part of the "Virginia Slims" women's tennis tournament. We had first started playing tennis and were not very skilled.

As luck would have it, Billy Jean King approached us asking if we could warm up with her. With much trepidation, Carl went on the other side of the net to return strokes with this tennis icon. Spectators flocked to the balcony to observe. Carl's racquet felt like it weighed 100 pounds! When Billy Jean went to the net to practice her volley, Carl was not skilled enough to direct each ball to her. Balls sailed past Billy Jean, but landed in the court. "Point", Tony exclaimed!

Chris Evert was sitting all by herself and Tony tried to goad Carl into sitting down and talking to her. As stated previously, he was much too shy and lacked the self-confidence to do so.

A celebrity tennis tournament was later held at the racquet club. Sunday's competitions were delayed for well over an hour when Rev. Jessie Jackson and actor-comedian Bill Cosby were protesting the tournament's limited access to people of color.

Another memory is of Carl attending a professional men's tennis tournament at Soldier Field. He was watching a singles match between Eddie Dibbs and an opponent whose name he cannot recall. Per Wikipedia: "Eddie attained a career-high singles ranking of world No. 5 in July 1978. Dibbs holds the record number of ATP Tour wins for a player who never reached a Grand Slam final."

A tremendous thunderstorm started in the middle of the match, continuing for over two hours. By the time the match restarted, Carl was literally the only fan in the stands. He moved down to the first row and was cheering loudly for Eddie. Eddie finally motioned Carl to come join him on the court, sitting on a chair alongside his. What a treat!

Lakeshore Racquet Club was owned by Jordon Kaiser. He also had owned the Chicago Cougars of the WHA (World Hockey Association) and the Chicago Aces of the newly formed

World Team Tennis Organization. We got to know Jordon well. His house bordered the 18th green at Glencoe's public golf course. He would often join us for a few holes. We would stake our accounting practice against his business interests.

Jordon often would complain that the World Team Tennis concept was not successful because of disagreements with another founding member, Lamar Hunt. Hunt was a founder of the AFL (American Football League) and the Kansas City Chiefs football team. When it appeared that we were close to defeat, we turned the conversation to Lamar Hunt; thereby derailing any hopes of a Jordon Kaiser victory.

By the time the 1976 Olympics rolled around, we had received our MBA degrees, Tony had married Anne, his supervisor at the accounting firm of Arthur (now Ernst &) Young & Company and Carl, after working for Price Waterhouse, had opened an accounting practice with Anne. Anne was pregnant with their first child, Carrie. Tony stayed at Arthur Young to get more experience and to provide a stable income for their family. The newly established practice sublet office space in the Wrigley Building from Mike Pyle, our friend and former Chicago Bears offensive captain.

Mitch Garner, Tony, Frank Shorter, Carl

As a result of Frank Shorter's win in 1972, the 1976 marathon took on more popularity. The race was heavily featured on television. Frank finished second to Waldemar Cierpinski of East Germany. After the fall of the Berlin Wall, documents were discovered implicating Cierpinski's involvement in a program that provided performance-enhancing drugs, or "PED's."

Thirty- three years later, Frank worked with President Clinton's White House staff to help create The United States Antidoping Agency and was chosen to be its first Chairman.

Frank was very gracious in his post-race interviews. Combined with his humility and the race being watched by a worldwide audience, Frank is generally credited with starting the running boom which is alive to this day. His accomplishments certainly inspired us to get back into running.

Shortly after beginning the CPA practice with Anne, Ruzicka & Associates, Carl called Frank at his home in Boulder, Colorado. It was a fortuitous call. Capitalizing on his fame, Frank was opening a retail running shop (Frank Shorter Sports) on Pearl Street in Boulder and his own running apparel manufacturing company (Frank Shorter Running Gear). He was looking for someone to help with his accounting needs. Ruzicka & Associates had one of its first major clients!

Frank Shorter Running Gear was first featured in the 1977 Trade Show at Chicago's McCormick Place. No one with the company was prepared for the first day's enormous interest from the suppliers and retailers. There existed only a small supply of sweat suits, running shorts, etc. That night, our Mom and Anne spent hours hurriedly sewing the company's label onto the apparel, and Tony went to the Arthur Young offices to xerox 500 flyers. What a night!

We believe that it was at the Trade Show the following year at McCormick Place that Frank left after the first few days to run the indoor two mile run at a track meet the upcoming Saturday evening in Albuquerque, New Mexico. The Friday night prior, we joined Frank in running approximately 200- meter intervals in McCormick's snow-covered parking lot. Frank had trouble keeping up with us for the first few. He stated that he could never get over our leg speed. Unfortunately, we had to run 18 more. We are certain that we somehow caught up to Frank after completion of the remaining intervals, as we drove him to the airport that night! That next night Frank set an American record in that indoor two-mile run!

Much later, we believe in 1989, Frank was part of the ESPN broadcasting team covering the Keebler Invitational in Elmhurst. This was an outdoor track meet featuring the best High School runners in the world. After the meet was finished, we began warming up on the track, while Frank was finishing up with voice over work for the telecast. He broadcast from the roof of the locker room.

Quizzically, he yelled down and asking what we were doing. We told him we were going to try to run 200 meters under 30 seconds. "No way!", he shouted, "you guys are way too fat!" As we were about to run, Frank had stopped his duties and we noticed that he was prepared to start his Casio stopwatch. Straining with every ounce of long, lost strength and speed we approached the finish line. Frank stopped his watch, 29 seconds! "Read it and weep"!

We evidently lived after our strenuous efforts, as we are now telling the story! It is most likely that we succeeded because Frank said we could not.

Frank was also a guest in the announcer's booth at a Cubs game. He was to be interviewed by the legendary Jack Brickhouse. Before heading up to the booth, we had Frank memorize some of Jack's favorite go-to expressions. "Look out now", "For just a hot minute there", "Oh Brother", "Oh Boy", "Hoo Wee", "Hey Hey", and others. During the interview Frank did his best to throw in as many of these expressions as possible. It was hilarious.

As the Olympics were reserved (theoretically) for amateurs, Frank embarked on trying to change running to a professional sport, one in which participants could accept appearance money and prize money. Frank testified to Congress and Olympic Committees to affect this change.

As his accountants, we were involved in part of the process. At the Hilton Hotel at O'Hare airport, we had a meeting with Frank; Olan Cassell, executive director of the AAU (Amateur Athletic Union); and Steve Bosley, president of the Bank of Boulder. A vehicle was set up in which the monies would go into trusts set up for the various athletes from which they would pay their personal expenses.

Herb Lindsay, one of the premier U.S. distance runners became the surrogate for Frank. Together with attorney Bob Stone, the initial trust was formed and called "The Herb Lindsay Amateur Trust". Bob along with his partner, Joe French, gave Frank his first job out of Law School working for their law firm French & Stone.

The trusts were soon bypassed as the runners received the money directly. In a small way, this paved the way for the Dream Team and others to make their Olympic appearances.

"Pay Day", the name of the trick or treat candy bar given to Frank, took on a different meaning!

It took some time (we wish that fact would sink into our skulls today), but we gradually got back into competition. Running along Chicago's lakefront, starting at Lake Shore Park at Chicago Ave., we were joined by Tom Boland, Bob Christiansen, Randy Seed and a former weightlifter, Reinhart (Nick) Nickich. On Sundays we would meet at Tony's house in Glencoe and run 20 miles throughout the North Shore suburbs.

Lake Shore Park is part of the Chicago Park District. The parks superintendents were Al Benedict and Don Jens. Al is credited with starting the popular "Chicago Air & Water Show". In 1977 he asked us if we wanted to go up in a F-16 fighter jet with the Blue Angels. We took a pass. We hoped to live another day and to continue our journey.

Bob Christiansen was a struggling artist who lived in the famed Tree Top Studios in the Medinah Temple building. All the runners befriended him and were sympathetic to his plight. At various races put on by Frank Shorter Sport retail stores, Bob was a consistent, post-race raffle winner of various Frank Shorter Running Gear apparel. Belying his Yale education, Tony once questioned how this could happen. Frank responded that any name pulled out of the hat became Bob Christiansen. Ah Hah!

One day, Bob received a letter from his old high school flame, Beatrice, in Muskegon, Michigan. She informed Bob that her husband had passed away and she was interested in getting together with him. Bob was reluctant to do so. We continually pestered him and finally goaded him to reply. Soon thereafter, Bob left Chicago to take care of his elderly father in Muskegon. His father died and we lost touch.

A few years ago, we researched Bob on the internet and came across his obituary. Bob died at age 88 in 2013, leaving behind his wife of 28 years, Beatrice. He had three step- children and one grandchild. Our persistence paid off. We had set him off on an improbable journey of his own!

While running along the lakefront, we were joined a few times by Tom O'Hara. Per Wikipedia, "Tom was the first native of the state of Illinois to break the four-minute mile barrier for the mile run when he ran 3:59.4 in 1963. He also held the world record for the fastest mile in indoor track, which was set when he ran 3:56.6 on February 13, 1964. He beat that record on March 6 of the same year with a time of 3:56.4, a world record that stood for fourteen years."

Tom graduated from St. Ignatius College Prep High School in Chicago, and then ran for Loyola University. He was setting records while the Loyola Ramblers were winning the 1963 NCAA Basketball Championship. We, along with friends Larry

Prochaska and Gary Jowers would listen to each game on the radio. The games were announced by Red Rush who famously would say, "Swisheroo, it goes right through", and when promoting the teams breadmaking sponsor urged us to "Get Gonnella, Fella".

Tom made it to the semi-finals at the 1964 Olympics. The gold medal winner was Peter Snell of New Zealand and the silver medal went to Josef Odlozil, from Czechoslovakia. A fellow countryman! We later met Josef when running at Yale. On those later runs we asked Tom why he did not perform up to his expectations. He said while in Tokyo he talked with Arthur Lydiard about his training techniques and ran himself into the ground trying to implement them. It seems like Arthur had adopted the strategy we used when playing golf with Jordon Kaiser: The old "psych job!"

Speaking of world records, we note that Tony is the unrecognized world record holder in the 40- yard dash. One evening a group of us runners ran intervals on Northwestern's outdoor track. We noticed that scouts were timing various football players in that distance. Tony asked to try. The scout told him to get down in a three- point stance and he would start his stopwatch when Tony lifted his hand off the ground. Tony ran the 40 yards in 0 (that is zero) seconds. He ran the distance with his hand still touching the ground! The scout had a good laugh, as did us runners!

On a few occasions, Alan Page and his wife joined us in our runs. Alan was a member of the "Purple People Eaters" of the Minnesota Vikings and a member of the Pro Football Hall of Fame. He had become a Chicago judge in his post NFL career and later the first African American Associate Justice of the State of Minnesota Supreme Court.

In 1979, Pope John Paul II became the first pope to visit Chicago. At that time, our office was located on the 16th floor of the Willoughby Towers, at 8 S. Michigan Avenue. Our office windows overlooked Michigan Ave and what is now Millennium Park. Many people of the Catholic faith asked if they could come and see the Pope as he came by. We happily complied. Unfortunately, the Pope mobile drove by in a complete blur. It was hardly worth the experience.

That night us runners took off for our nightly workout. For a reason that we cannot remember, we chose to run on the inner path leading to North Ave. Within a matter of minutes, the Pope passed us on his way to Cardinal Cody's mansion. We were all within 5 to 10 feet of the Pope! The Pope gave us his blessing from the Pope mobile!

The superintendent of Willoughby Towers was Louie Klemanovic. Mike Krzyzewski (Coach "K") of Duke basketball and "March Madness" fame was Louie's nephew. Coach K's mother and Louie's wife were sisters. Louie and his wife Virginia were wonderful people with kind hearts and quick wit. Our parents enjoyed seeing Louie when visiting our office. We were thrilled when Louie wore the latest Duke apparel sent by his nephew.

While officing at 8 S. Michigan Ave., we befriended three homeless individuals asking for assistance most mornings and afternoons as we walked to or from our office and the Monroe Street parking garage. They were James, Kenny, and Ernie.

We were able to secure a job for James unloading trucks at McCormick Place. James was a large man. When inquiring as to his progress on the job, he states his feet hurt from the heavy carrying. His old shoes were worn down to paper thin soles. "No problem", we said, "let's go and get some new shoes". Unfortunately, this was not a simple task. James shoe size was 16 ½.

We also secured a job for Kenny as a messenger. This too presented certain challenges. He needed a bike, a helmet, and a lock for the bike.

We learned that being homeless presented challenges that were not readily apparent.

One day, arriving at our office around 6:00 in the evening,

Carl decided to treat James to a hamburger at the Burger King restaurant on Michigan Ave. Inside, James and Carl encountered Tony and Kenny, who were doing the same thing. We all enjoyed a good laugh!

Ernie had been a boxer in the Golden Gloves. We told him about attending the tournament as youngsters with our father. At that time, we wore business suits to work. One evening, Tony and Ernie were shadow boxing on the corner of Michigan and Monroe Avenues. Passersby wondered why a businessman and homeless individual were duking it out in broad daylight!

In 1994, Carrie wanted to run the Chicago Marathon and Tony agreed to pace her. The marathon route ran past our office and then into various Chicago neighborhoods. Tony tied his car keys to his shoelaces for safekeeping. As luck would have it, Tony's shoe came untied and the keys were lost.

After the race, he and Carrie decided to go to our office to have the building manager call their home so that Anne could pick them up. On their way to the office they crossed the street and there lying in front of them were the car keys!

Soon we all began running various races held on the lakefront. Our Mom and Dad became fixtures at the races. We can still hear our Mom: "Why do you want us here? Just so we can hold your sweat clothes?" Our parents became fast friends with our fellow runners for more important reasons. They cheered their support and took part in many of our social gatherings, offering advice and imparting knowledge with humor and care.

We ran to Bruce Springsteen's "Born To Run" and sang "Let's Get Physical" by Olivia Newton John.

When in town, Frank Shorter would join the whole group for our runs along the lakefront. Word spread quickly of our friendship, and various members of the running community solicited us to get Frank to run in some of their races. One of these runners was Wendell Miller, a founding member of Club North Shore in Lake Bluff. Frank became a regular at the First National

Bank 20K race. One year, Frank ran with us in the Glencoe fun run held every Fourth of July. The participants and cheerleading family members could not believe it!

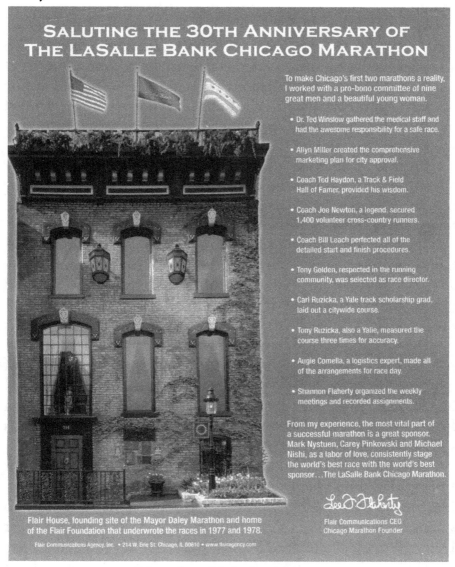

Marathon 30th Anniversary

Wendell Miller was also an acquaintance of Lee Flaherty, founder and CEO of Flair Communications. Lee formed a pro-bono committee to organize Chicago's first marathon. Because of our reputation as Frank Shorter's friends, we were asked to be on the committee. This started our involvement with the Chicago Marathon.

As accountants we were tasked with paying the bills, depositing entry fee dollars, and providing financial statements. We also designed and measured the course. In addition, we used our friendships to invite famous runners who we hosted at our homes. Our memory is that the budget for the marathon, funded in its entirety by Flair Communications and runners' entry fees was very modest with $10,000 budgeted for invited runners.

The first year or so the race was called the "Mayor Daley Marathon" in honor of the first Richard J Daley, who was mayor of Chicago from 1955 until his death in December 1976. The first race was held on September 25, 1977.

The second marathon created quite a stir. Per Wikipedia and Chicagotribune.com., "the marathon was run in controversy after race founder Lee Flaherty doubled the entry fee to $10 and moved the starting time from 8 to 10:30 a.m. so that more of the city would be awake to watch the race."

The race date was September 24, 1978 and the temperature rose to 82.3 degrees. It was a borderline disaster. As a result of that race, Beatrice Foods, then a corporate conglomerate based in Chicago, took over sponsorship and CARA (Chicago Area Runners Association) was organized in protest. Lee Flaherty was still heavily involved.

Tony ran the Boston Marathon in 1978, wearing a Major Daley Marathon t-shirt. His legs cramped up coming down Heartbreak hill, and he almost crawled to the finish. A not too sympathetic spectator offered him these words: "You're Mayor Daley all right, you're dead"!

The 1979 marathon was pushed back to October, but it turned out to be another extremely hot day.

To help diffuse the criticisms of the 1978 and 1979 experiences, we proposed that 100% of the entry fee money for the

1980 race be earmarked for charity. There were 4500 entrants and a check written to the Chicago Boys Club for about $45,000.

At the follow up marathon committee meeting, we stated that this was great, but we could do much better. What did the Boys Club do for this money? They should get sponsors. The participants should get sponsors. We would like to think that, in not so small of a way, we planted the seed for the business of "running for philanthropy."

In 2019, the marathon raised a record $27.1 million for charity. Ruzicka & Associates' largest client, the AIDS Foundation of Chicago, has been a major recipient.

Through our running and marathon involvement we became acquaintances, then friends with Michael Bilandic, who succeeded Richard J. Daley as mayor of Chicago. He was a wonderful man and a fellow Croatian.

One day around lunch time, out of the blue, we decided to go see Mayor Bilandic at his 4th floor City of Chicago Office. The receptionist and other staff members were incredulous. "No way can one just appear without an appointment and see the Mayor". We asked them if they would at least let him know we were there. After begrudgingly making the call, the receptionist looked shocked. "Wait a few minutes and the Mayor will see you." We were escorted in and had a nice, short conversation. The Mayor called in the office photographer who took our picture with the Mayor. The Ruzicka twins strike again!

Carl, Mayor Michael Bilandic, Tony

On one run with the Mayor, he asked how far we were going to run. We replied about ten miles to Irving Park and back. He insisted we only run to Belmont. Tony jokingly replied, "Who died and left you boss?"

Largely, because of his lack of action after the great Chicago blizzard of 1978, Mayor Bilandic lost the next election and was replaced by Jane Byrne. Mayor Bilandic would occasionally join us for runs along the lakefront. On one such venture, Tony stated that it was too bad that there was a blizzard. He quickly replied, "It wasn't the snow!" It never was a topic of conversation thereafter.

Like Mayor Daley, Mayor Bilandic lived in Bridgeport, an area just south of downtown Chicago. It was once inhabited by Irish and Italian immigrant families, but now has a large Chinese population.

On one run heading north along the lake, he asked "what do you know about that building?" We replied, "We think that's 1212 N. Lake Shore Drive. We have a few clients that live there." After another few steps, he asked the same question. "That is 1400 N. Lake Shore Drive, we have a few clients there too". We asked, "are you thinking of moving from Bridgeport?" He replied, "I never said that!" Shortly thereafter it became news when he and his wife Heather Morgan Bilandic moved to a near north Lake Shore Drive residence.

Twice a year, we would receive a call from Mayor Bilandic's secretary to meet him for lunch at the Monroe Harbor Yacht Club. It was time to reset his Casio watch forward or back to allow for the time changes of Central Daylight time.

Every year we were "flies in the ointment" in the marathon meetings. The first year of Mayor Byrne's tenure, we went to her office with Beatrice Foods personnel to secure dates for that year's marathon. The date could not coincide with a Chicago Bears home game or other planned events. Beatrice personnel would walk in the office very timidly with their "hat in hand", prepared to accept whatever date was offered. After exiting the Mayor's office, we asked them what were they doing? We should present the marathon from a position of strength. We are serving as an economic engine for the City.

At one heated meeting at Beatrice, security was summoned, and we were escorted out of their office. We would share our frustrations with our running friends. One night at a party at Tom Boland's home, his partner Herb Levy asked, "why do you put yourselves through such pain and anguish?"

In 2018, the marathon contributed a record breaking $378 million to the city's economy and $328 million in 2017.

We also called for substantial increases in the budget to bring in runners. Many of the featured runners we had met through Frank Shorter. They would participate for free, stay at our homes, and eat our prepared meals.

One of these runners was Steve Flanagan. Steve was an excellent runner, just a notch below our country's elite, and a treasured friend. His then wife, Cheryl Flanagan Bridges once held the American and world record in the marathon. Their daughter is Shalane Flanagan who has won the New York City Marathon and won a silver medal in the 10,000- meter run at the 2008 Olympics in Beijing.

Quoting Wikipedia, "In the 2018 Chicago Marathon, the total purse distributed among all the money winners is $803,500. There are bonuses for course records: $75,000 for men and women; and $5,000 for the wheelchair division." This was in addition to appearance money, travel, meals, and lodging.

The night before the 1981 Chicago Marathon, Frank Shorter was staying with Tony and Anne in Glencoe. They had their second child, Annette, in January earlier that year. After dinner, we went to buy baby bottles. Frank would use his own bottles at the water stations. He would cut the nipple and fill the bottles with Coca Cola after shaking out the carbonation. We decided to drive the bottles to the person in charge of the water station that night. The following morning, we were to be on the lead truck in front of the runners, as we were the only ones that knew the intricacies of the course.

It had been raining the entire day and Carl was driving a little too fast for conditions. Our car hit some standing water in the left lane of the Kennedy Expressway around Diversey Avenue, hydroplaning against the inner guard rail. We decided that we would straighten out the car and assess the damage when we arrived downtown. The car was perpendicular to the traffic. Tony said to be careful while backing up and straightening the car as cars were swerving around us. It was too late. We looked to our left to see a car heading right towards us.

We were both awakened by paramedics straddled over us and shining a light in our eyes. Carl was in the driver's seat and Tony in the right back seat. The paramedics asked us, "Where are you going? Where are you coming from? Do you know what happened?" We did not have a clue. We stated that we must have been in some type of accident.

Tony asked, "What about the other people in the car?" They responded that there were no other people. He asked, "How about the baby?" They responded there was no baby. We could not figure out why Tony was in the backseat and why there were baby bottles. Did something happen to Annette?

Lastly, we asked about the other car. "There is no other car." We were involved in a hit and run accident. We often wonder if we would have been able to state our names if asked. We were taken to St. Joseph's hospital via ambulance.

As we were to be on the lead truck the next morning, we signed ourselves out of the hospital. This was necessitated because hospital protocol required an overnight observation period from patients who had been concussed. The next day, although rather severely injured, we were in the lead truck.

This accident, combined with our frustrations over lack of a proper budget and foresight into what the marathon could mean to the City of Chicago, resulted in our presenting our ideas rather angrily to the committee. Our involvement with the marathon ended shortly thereafter.

There was one incident, however, that we found humorous in the 1981 marathon. Race day communications were the responsibility of "West Suburban React". They were represented by a group of individuals that spoke a language of their own. One of the member's first name was Jerry. At the numerous meetings leading up to the race, Jerry always attended. At the last pre-race meeting held to go over final race details, the "React" team emphasized the need to have vehicles that possessed cigarette lighters. The CB radio equipment would be plugged into the cigarette lighter feature in the car.

At the postrace meeting, West Suburban React complained vehemently that certain of the rented vehicles did not have cigarette lighters and they had to hot wire them to use the CB equipment. Jerry was not at the meeting. We were told that Jerry was sick. In our effort to lighten the discussion, we asked about Jerry. We were told that he had bypass surgery, had a pacemaker installed, and that as long as its battery held up, Jerry would be ok. Tony replied, "I sure hope his car has a cigarette lighter"!

We are proud to have developed friendships with other tremendous runners. They include: Francie Larrieu Smith, who participated in four straight Olympics, running events ranging from 800 meters to the marathon. She was the flagbearer for the 1992 Olympic team; Herb Lindsay, who was named Road Racer of the year for consecutive years by Runners' World Magazine and remains the record holder in the one hour run; Ellen Hart, women Road Runner of the year for two consecutive years; and Gordon Minty, from Wales, a member of Eastern Michigan University's Hall of Fame. Although he was not nearly the caliber of these runners, we enjoyed running with Bill Mueller who ran one of Frank Shorter's retail stores.

We runners ran a lot of miles. We often discussed our limited stretching before workouts and races. Gordon Minty put it best, "You don't see the horses leaning up against the wall before their races!" Unfortunately, we are paying the price today. Can you say, "stiff as a board"?

In a 2015 get together, Herb Lindsay stated that the runners could not get over our accomplishments as we "had jobs"! Given our size, we also were at somewhat of a disadvantage. When going for a recent 7 mile walk with his taller wife Qian Yi, Carl's fitness app showed he walked 19,000 steps. Qian Yi's app showed 17,000!

While racing in high school for the CTA track club we ran a 15- kilometer race featuring Hal Higdon. Hal is a major contributor to "Runners World" and has written many books on running. He is one of the founders of the Road Runners Club of America. Much later, we ran the Hal Higdon half marathon in Indiana. Sleeping at his house on the night before the race, everyone was kept awake as Bob Christiansen snored and Carl whimpered in his sleep.

We also met George Hirsch, founder of the New York Marathon, founding publisher of the "Runner" magazine, and first publishing director of "Men's Health" magazine.

We were guests of Frank at a local luncheon sponsored by "Sports Illustrated". We were introduced to Tony Trabert, former tennis star, author and commentator, and Johnny Klippstein, a former major league pitcher with various teams, including the Cubs. This was a real coup! He was our brother and Uncle Tom's favorite in the early 1950's!

Along with Dave Glasssman, proprietor of the "Park West" nightclub located in the near north side, we helped organize the first Chicago Sports Fitness Expo at the convention center in Rosemont. Participants included Frank Shorter; Peggy Fleming, Olympic figure skating champion and commentator; and Arnold Schwarzeneggar. Arnold was far and away the most popular attraction. Frank was a very distant second. "Hasta la vista, baby"!

Through David, Tony was able to meet rock & roll icon, David Bowie. Tony seemed to be in his own "Space Oddity"!

Tony later met Mick Jagger while running at the East Bank Club. He resisted the impulse of singing "Time is On My Side", one of our themes as high school runners. Carl met Gene Pitney, another early rock & roll star while running at Lake Shore Park. Unlike Tony with Mick, Carl regaled Gene with a few bars of "It Hurts to be in Love", "The Man Who Shot Liberty Valance", and "24 Hours From Tulsa"! Gene Pitney was at the stage of his career that he was just happy that someone had remembered.

Lee Flaherty hosted a party after one of the first Chicago Marathons. At a party we met Phil Donahue famous TV talk show host, and his wife, Marlo Thomas, daughter of comedian Danny Thomas, and star of the TV series "That Girl", which ran from 1966 to 1971. We told her that her dad's television show, "Make Room for Daddy" was one of our favorites. We jokingly inquired as to the health of "Uncle Tannous", a character on that show played by Hans Conried.

At this party we first met Harry Caray. Harry was the legendary broadcaster for many baseball teams. Most notably he was the TV announcer for the Cubs. He gained national fame when promoting one of the team's sponsors, Budweiser Beer. He would proclaim, "I'm Cubs Fan and A Bud Man". His call of a Cubs home run is part of Cubs lore, "It could be, it might be, it is! Holy Cow!"

At another marathon function, we met Scott Brady, the star of the TV series we watched as children, "Shotgun Slade". We will never forget our salutation, "How you doin Shotgun?"

One year, Tony and his family went to the Honolulu Marathon. Frank Shorter was the featured runner. A large contingent of Japanese spectators were there. Frank had previously won the Fukuoka Marathon four straight times from 1971 to 1974. The Japanese crowded him for autographs. Tony's daughter Carrie had light blond hair at the time and the Japanese were fascinated.

They showed Carrie great attention, prompting her to exclaim, "I must be some kind of autograph person!"

At the marathon, Tony met singer Don Ho and Jack Lord, the famous actor of the original "Hawaii Five-O" television series. "Book him Danno!"

Through Frank, we were able to meet Kihachiro Onitsuka, founder of the Asics Tiger running shoe company. We were introduced to the Japanese custom of presenting one's business card with the name and company facing out and presented with a bow. Mr. Onitsuka did not ask Carrie for her autograph.

We attended the last three days of track & field events at the 1984 Olympics held in Los Angeles with our good friend and staff member Mike Scardina. We stayed with our Mom's oldest brother, Uncle Nick, who was living in Duarte. We took the train and/or bus from nearby Pasadena to the Coliseum. The fare was paid with a small gold color token.

Frank was only able to secure us tickets for Thursday's morning session. For other events we were on our own. We quickly learned that some patrons had bought full day track & field passes but were going to attend other sport venues in the evening session. We would then ask them if we could have their passes. This resulted in an Olympic event of its own. We would use those passes to barter with scalpers, either upgrading to better tickets, or negotiating downward to cheaper seats. This allowed us to pay for other sessions. In this short span of three days, we all became friends and greeted each other with, "Are you holdin?"

After one evening session, while walking outside the Coliseum on our way to the train, we heard "Ruzicka" yelled from behind us. It was Bill Rodgers, famous marathoner. We explained pleasantries and told him that we had won the gold medal, proudly displaying our train tokens!

One night, Tony called home to speak with his daughters. Carrie was now 7 years old and Annette was 3. They asked him to bring them some medals. Tony told them it would not be fair to the athletes who had worked so hard to accomplish their dreams. Nevertheless, they asked Tony to bring back any "extras". Tony told Annette that he would bring home a gold medal, and she asked, "what color is it?" Both were excited about joining us for the next Olympic games. Tony explained that would be difficult as the games were to be held in South Korea. They said that was okay. "We'll all stay with Uncle Nicky"!

We had met two of the world's greatest woman marathoners, Greta Waitz, from Sweden and Rosa Mota, from Portugal. While arriving to line up for the 1985 New York Marathon in which we were to pace our brother Tom, we were greeted by their voices yelling to us using the true pronunciation of our name, "Roo zheech ka!" This remains a thrill.

The three Ruzicka brothers regaled an unsuspecting taxi driver with stories of Chicago. The gentleman became our wakeup call the morning of the race, and our personal driver for the entire weekend. He asked that he pick us up early for our trip to the airport the following day. We had to stop for a famous "Coney Island" hot dog!

In our last years of running, we began running at the Multiplex in Deerfield. The Bulls held their workouts there before the Berto Center was built. We often showered with the team and Michael Jordon would always say "Here comes the speedsters"!

Michael, of course, called us "Twin."

When watching the Bulls playoff runs with our Mom, Carl often complained that the players seemed to be ignoring Toni Kukoc, a fellow Croatian. Our Mom parroted the complaint. Sometime in that time frame, she admitted to not being able to see the players faces or numbers on the big screen.

For our 30th birthday, a best friend, George Kriaris spray painted a pair of his wife Barbara's orthopedic shoes yellow and added red racing stripes. He gave them to Tony as an old person's running shoes. Tony loves the shoes as they have a slight heal wedge adding height!! Tony wears them dancing. A client, the

Illinois Humanities Council would have an annual holiday party which included a grab bag exchange of gifts to be followed by bowling.

Tony had a history of getting a special gift for one staff member, E. J. Hendricks. Each year he would gift her gloves or a scarf. One year, Tony decided to wear the shoes to the holiday party as he could also wear them while bowling. The Council's office was at 17 N. State Street just south of Macy's. Tony realized he had not purchased the gift for E.J. and wearing the shoes went to Macy's. While at the checkout counter, he noticed large lines behind him.

As he turned, he noticed actress Raquel Welch on a platform perhaps only six feet away. She was there signing perfume bottles. Raquel saw Tony and commented, "Nice shoes". That was the only time Tony wore the shoes downtown. He certainly impressed the right person!

In 1989, we went to New York to run with Frank Shorter in a college alumni race sponsored by Alamo Rent A Car. Following the pre-race banquet, we hailed a taxi for our trip back to our hotel. Coming out of the taxi we were about to enter was David Letterman. He was wearing a Cubs hat and jacket!

Later Tony and his family took a walk in Central Park where they met William Atherton, star of Tony's daughters' favorite movies, "Real Genius" and "Ghostbusters". It is quite possible that Tony's daughters, stealing a line from "Real Genius", asked, "is that your real hair?"

In 2013, Frank came to Chicago for Tony's daughter Carrie's wedding and reception. On Saturday he decided to go for a short run. Tony asked how fast he would be running. Frank replied, "Barely discernable from a walk!" We joined him. Our nephew, Andrew also came along. With visions of grandeur, Andrew could not believe that he had "beaten" an Olympic marathon gold medal winner. Andrew's younger brother Jack later ran for his school's cross country team.

In 2018, Carl entered the YWCA of Evanston/Northshore 10K. Instead of punching his Casio watch at the start of the race, Carl should have timed himself with a sun dial. Proudly, he started and finished on the same day!

We remain best of friends with Frank to this day. In Frank's autobiography "My Marathon, Reflections on a Gold Medal Life", he states:

"Carl and Tony Ruzicka are fast and true friends from Yale. A couple of good people who have always had my best interests at heart, financially and otherwise. They are not afraid to advise me, even in the toughest way, and I always trust their judgement."

We can say the same thing about Frank. In an October 2011 issue of "Runners World" magazine, Frank broke a lifelong silence about childhood abuse at the hands of his doctor father. That we had already known this for years, symbolizes the depth of our friendship.

During this whole wonderful journey, our true first love was the Chicago Cubs. We have mentioned Yosh Kawano and made other Cubs references. Now is time to tell stories of this love affair!

THE CHICAGO CUBS EXPERIENCE

W E WERE FORTUNATE TO HAVE our older brother Tom take us to a few Cubs games early in our lives. We would rush up the bleacher ramp, smell the outfield grass, soak in the sunshine and wait for Pat Piper (long time Cubs field announcer) to give us the lineups over the loud speaker, "Attention, attention please, get your pencils and scorecards ready and I will give you the correct lineup for today's ballgame". All the kids did their best (worst) to imitate him.

One Christmas, we learned where our presents were being hid. When our parents were away, we hurriedly went through the bag of pre-wrapped gifts. We got new baseball gloves! Tom caught us in the act. After admonishing us for opening everything up, he wanted to know if there were any new record albums included in the bag! Our Mom and Dad never noticed that when taking the gloves out of their wrapped boxes, they were already worked in with a perfect pocket!

We devoured every sport book, especially a series of baseball books by John R. Tunis, including "The Kid From Tomkinsville" and "Highpockets." The books' characters became the Cubs players, or maybe the Islanders, or just maybe the Ruzicka twins. We memorized "Pass That Puck!" by Richard T. Flood. At the library, we scoured the 920 series of the Dewey Decimal System for sport biographies.

As Christmas or birthday presents, we received books written by Tom Meany including books on the Yankees, the Brooklyn Dodgers, and the Milwaukee Braves and "Baseballs Greatest Players." We read "Batboy of the Giants", by Garth Gareu, and imagined ourselves in the lead role. Little did we know that we are now writing a similar book about our Chicago Bears experiences!

A favorite book was "The Pros: A Documentary of Professional Football in America." The book was published in 1960 with Tex Maule and Robert Riger as its authors. The book's focus was on the 1958 NFL Championship game. This game was won in overtime by the Baltimore Colts who defeated the New York Giants. We took turns being Johnny Unitas and Raymond Berry. Sometimes we were Lenny Moore.

Photography and artwork were provided by Robert Riger. An entire section of the book was devoted to his artistic renderings of the pioneers of football. As budding artists, we simply loved this book.

The following Christmas, we asked our parents to give us the book's sequel as a present. Surely, they would come through. We were down to our last present. it was a book! Literally crying out in disappointment, the book was not the one hoped for. Rather, it was "The Scoring Twins: A Story of Biddy Basketball". Our tears flowed.

The book is about the friendship that grows between two youngsters from "different sides of the track." It became our absolute favorite. Parents know best!

That book, the humility shown by Cecil McDade the hero in "Highpockets", and other books read help shape our lessons in tolerance and friendships. Perhaps it was through these narratives that we were not threatened by the diverse background of students of Yale, but instead embraced and learned from the different socio-economic differences.

Each Christmas morning, we children would rush into the living room to see what presents Santa had left on late Christmas Eve. We could not understand how our Uncle Bill, sleeping on the living room sofa, did not hear Santa. The festivities started with our Dad playing the "Mario Lanza Christmas Album" on the family Victrola turntable.

For the years 1958 to 1960 or so, we were also gifted Hartland baseball statues. These were lifelike plastic figurines about 8 ½ inches tall of some of baseball's greatest players. Statues of Babe Ruth, Ted Williams, Stan Musial, Willie Mays, Yogi Berra, Mickey Mantle, Hank Aaron, Warren Spahn, Eddie Matthews, Duke Snider, Don Drysdale, Nellie Fox, and our beloved Ernie Banks remain in our possession. Like all collectibles, we realize the value is in the memories of our first tearing apart the Christmas or birthday wrappings to see what player had been bestowed to us.

Our brother Tom taught us how to play every sport. We were also fortunate that our Uncle Tom was such a Cubs historian and excellent athlete. He threw a double curve. More accurately, the ball curved, then straightened out. His next- door neighbor, a scientist, argued this was against the law of physics. Uncle Tom would throw this pitch to us batters. We would reach to hit the curve, only to be clonked in the head. Let the neighbor try it!

We were also fortunate that our brother Tom let us stay after the game to get autographs. We would each buy a scorecard and wait for the players to depart Wrigley Field. Getting player autographs was exciting and very meaningful for us

In our youth, visiting players were most accessible as the path from the visitors' clubhouse to the dugout took the players down steps protected by an iron fence which one could put their arm through with a baseball or scorecard for signature. After the game, the team bus waited outside on the parkway north of Addison and just west of Sheffield. We did not leave the ballpark until it seemed to be devoid of living people!

The first scorecard in our collection was a game held August 31, 1957 against the St. Louis Cardinals. With taxes included, prices were $2.50 for box seats, $1.25 for grandstand, and $.60 for bleachers. For children under 14 the prices were reduced to $1.85 for box seats and $.60 for grandstand, respectively. A hot dog cost $.25 and Coca Cola $.15. Pabst Blue Ribbon beer cost $.35!! Cubs caps cost $1.00 and jackets cost $7.95. The scorecard cost $.10.

One of our most prized possessions is the scorecard of the game held August 23, 1958 versus the Pittsburgh Pirates. Grandstand seats for adults were now $.75 and bleacher seats had skyrocketed to $.75, however smaller cokes were now offered at $.15. On this scorecard we have autographs of many outstanding Pirates, including Roberto Clemente (Hall of Fame Member), Bill Virdon (1955 National League Rookie of the Year and future manager of the Pirates, Yankees, and Astros), Bob Friend, Vernon Law and Elroy Face. Gino Cimoli, an outfielder also signed the card.

Carl later drew a picture of Gino and sent it to him. Gino replied with an autographed picture postcard mailed from San Francisco dated Nov. 12, 1960. On which he wrote "Thank you for the wonderful drawing."

Occasionally, we take the card out and show our friends. These players were stars of the 1960 World Series! Yet, our biggest kick is that we got Danny Kravitz (an obscure 3rd string catcher)! Us twins did not play favorites when collecting autographs. Anyone wearing a uniform or looking like a ballplayer was fair game.

We also have the scorecard of the game versus the San Francisco Giants September 6, 1958 autographed by Alvin Dark and Tony Taylor of the Cubs and Al Worthington, Daryl Spencer, and Don Johnson of the inaugural 1958 Giants team in San Francisco.

Not to leave out the 1958 first Dodgers team in Los Angeles, we have a scorecard of the game held September 20 or 21, 1958. Signatures include Dale Long (1st player to homerun in 8 consecutive games-to be later joined by Ken Griffey, Jr. and Don Mattingly), and Bobby Thomson (yes **the** Bobby Thomson, then on the New York Giants, who hit the "Shot Heard 'Round the World", a homerun to beat the Dodgers in the 1951 playoff game. The home run was hit off of Ralph Branca.

For some reason 1959 and 1960 are skipped. Perhaps it was because our mother most likely did not allow us to ride the "L" train by ourselves until we were 12 years old. Maybe it was because our brother Tom, now a star dancer on Chicago Bandstand, was too busy dating to take us to games.

We do have the ticket stub from Don Cardwell's no-hitter pitched May 15, 1960. It was one of the few games when our Dad and his three sons went together to a game.

As a result of Tom's dancing appearances, we both became interested in rock and roll music at an early age. We would go down to the basement to "spin some 45's". We sang along to "Don't Be Cruel" and " I want You, I Need You, I love You" by Elvis Presley; "All I Have To Do Is Dream" by the Everly Brothers; "We Got Love" by Bobby Rydell; and "Sweet Little Sixteen" by Chuck Berry.

Another scorecard is from a game held June 29, 1961 against the Cincinnati Reds. The Reds lost to the New York Yankees in the 1961 World Series. The only change in ticket prices was an increase in adult grandstand seats from $1.50 to $1.51!! Adult size Cubs jackets were now $9.95 while children's sizes remained at $7.95.

That day we learned that the scouts sat behind home plate and are thus included in our autographs. The most famous of the scouts include Art Stewart, Johnny Mostil, and Chuck Koney The most famous signature on this scorecard is Rogers Hornsby. Rogers Hornsby is in the Hall of Fame. He is considered the greatest right-handed hitter of all-time. His lifetime batting average of .358 is second only to Ty Cobb at .367. Hornsby is the only player to hit 40 home runs and hit over .400 in the same season. He holds the single season highest batting average of .424.

A July 1961 Cubs scorecard includes the autograph of Cuno Barragan, a rookie catcher for the Cubs. He had just gotten off the disabled list after breaking his ankle in spring training. While getting his autograph, Carl accidentally stepped on it. Cuno yelled out in pain! Fortunately, Cuno was ok.

Cuno was one of a list of less than stellar Cubs catchers we cheered for: Harry Chiti, Hobie Landrith, Elvin Tappe, Moe Thacker, Cal Neeman , Meritt Ranew, Randy Lee Bobb, and Vic Raznofsky, are names that immediately come to mind.

Never mind their stats, we loved them all! Who could not get excited when Darcy Ray Fast threw to Randy Lee Bobb?

Another interesting scorecard is a game against the Giants, August 14, 1962. This scorecard is autographed by Hall of Famers Willie Mays and Willie McCovey as well as Billy Pierce, Jose Pagan, Stu Miller, Felipe Alou, and Hank Sauer. Box seats now cost $3.00 for adults and $2.00 for children under 14.

A scorecard of the game June 21, 1963 against the Pirates is autographed by Hall of Fame member Willie Stargell as well as Professional Football Hall of Fame member Willie Davis, defensive end of the Green Bay Packers. We "sniffed him out" sitting in the box seats at Wrigley. Willie later received his master's degree in business administration from the University of Chicago.

As we get reacquainted with each scorecard or autograph, we revert back to our wonderful experiences: dutifully scoring the card as taught by our brother Tom, waiting for the players to come out, elbowing fellow autograph seekers, and reliving the game when we got home as the scorecard told the story.

There are so many instances that stand out in our memory:

We attended the game in 1958, when Dale Long became the

first left-handed throwing catcher since 1902. We are not sure which name applies to which incident, but either Moe Thacker or Cal Neeman started the game. One was injured and the other one ejected. Thus, another piece of Cubs history witnessed by the Ruzicka twins!

In 1959, we wrote the Cubs a letter asking them to bench second baseman Tony Taylor and replace him with Earl Averill, Jr. We received a reply form William Wrigley III, stating that it was important to have defense up the middle and have team speed. Taylor would remain in the lineup.

Taylor went on to have an excellent 19 years career. He played primarily for the Philadelphia Phillies and was a two time all-star. His career WAR (wins above replacement is 23.2. Averill, Jr. had a seven years career with a WAR of 3.6.

Luckily, we did a better job designing the Bears defense to stop the shotgun offense in 1961!

Somehow, we learned that the Detroit Tigers (in town to play the White Sox) were having their post-game party at the "Old Prague" restaurant, the most popular of many restaurants serving Czech food in Cicero. The restaurant was only a few blocks from our house. We crashed the party to get the autographs of Al Kaline, Hall of Fame member; Frank Lary, a great pitcher known as the "Yankee Killer"; and others.

We are reasonably certain that we did not scoop up a helping of pork, dumplings, and sauerkraut in the process.

The players signed a 1959 Chicago White Sox scorebook. White Sox Hall of Fame second baseman Nellie Fox also signed the program. The scorebook is multipage with numerous adver-tisements unlike the Cubs scorecard. Later, we drew a picture of Nellie Fox and presented it to him on "Nellie Fox Day" at Comiskey Park.

In 1960, the Cubs exchanged managers and radio announc-ers. Lou Boudreau went from the radio booth to manager and Charlie Grimm from manager to announcer. The announcement said that Lou would hold a practice with the Cubs the next day at Wrigley. Lou Boudreau was from Harvey, Illinois, a suburb south of Chicago, and he still lived there. The 22nd Place gang immediately went to work. We found his listing in the phone book, called him, and he invited us to the practice.

With pure excitement, we made our way to Wrigley, found our way in, started our walk up the tunnel to the field, heard the beautiful sound of bat hitting ball and walked up the last ramp to see the field. Almost at our last step, we were met by Harry "New York" Hazlewood, who shouted, "Get outta here"! What a disappointment.

Harry was the long- time caretaker at Wrigley. Later he became a tax client.

In 1960, our Sunday school teacher, Jim Forbes took our class to a Sox game after church. We sat in box seats perhaps in the 5th row or so. In those years Wally Phillips of channel 9 TV hosted a pregame show "Fan in the Stand". Wally was on the field, saw us twins, and asked us to be on the show. Wally's question to each of us was simple: if we were managers of the Sox, what changes would we make to improve the team?

We replied that we would replace Luis Aparicio (future Hall of Famer) with Sammy Esposito (a career .207 hitter), replace Jim Landis (speedy center fielder) with Earl Torgeson (an aging, slow 37 year old first baseman) to take advantage of Earl's speed, and pitch Mike Garcia (once an excellent pitcher now past his prime at age 37 with a record of 0-0) every third day.

Wally remarked that we "had been in the sun too long".

Our appearance was the rage of Terry Hrabak and other Cubs fan friends. It was met with disdain by Dale Bernard, Larry Prochaska, and other friends who cheered for the White Sox.

We suffered through the Cubs "'College of Coaches" in 1961and 1962, making sure that we procured the autograph of each coach: Bobby Adams, Rip Collins, Alvin Dark, Bob Kennedy, Charlie Metro, Buck O'Neil, Vedie Himsl, and others.

Per Wikipedia, Buck O'Neil "was a player and manager in the Negro American League, mostly with the Kansas City Monarchs. Buck became the first African American Coach in Major League Baseball. He played a major role in establishing the Negro Leagues Baseball Museum in Kansas City, Missouri. On December 7, 2006, he was posthumously awarded the Presidential Medal of Freedom by President George W. Bush.

Vedie Himsl, became a scout and then Director of Scouting for the Cubs. He became one of our first clients when we started our own accounting practice.

Lew Fonseca and John Hennessy of the Cubs also became our clients. Lew was a Cubs hitting instructor and one of the first to use film in analyzing baseball games and finding flaws in players. John was a longtime scout. His most successful signing was Joe Giradi, a catcher with the Cubs and former manager of the Florida Marlins and New York Yankees. Joe currently manages the Philadelphia Phillies.

In the early days of Ruzicka & Associates, we would always ask John to bring the speed gun to time our fastballs. Over the years John would say the gun had been given to another scout, or he could not find it, or the gun was broken. Finally, John called excitedly that he had the gun and was ready for action. Unfortunately, we were then 50 years old!

Of course, we would still follow the Cubs on WGN TV and WGN radio. We watched and/or listened to Jack Brickhouse, Jack Quinlan, Vince Lloyd, and Lou Boudreau. Home runs were hit over the "Tru Link fence"; we were encourage to buy our shoes at O'Connor and Goldberg, "Oh Gee, Oh Yah"; and buy Serta mattresses, "that's Serta, S E R T A".

On July 30, 1962, our brother Tom took all of us kids to the All-Star game. We arrived at the ballpark by 6:00 A.M., hoping to get our usual seats in the front row of the right field bleachers. Unfortunately, there already were many fans. Lines stretched along both the right field and left field outer walls, waiting for the gates to open. Tom had the brilliant idea of moving us right to the center. That ticket taker location had never been used before. Not that day. That was the first area to open for business. We could always count on our older brother!

To our dismay, and the delight of our Sox fan friends, The American League won the 9-4. To rub it in Luis Aparicio completed two double plays, Ray Herbert of the White Sox was the winning pitcher and powerless Pet Runnels of the Red Sox hit a home run. Pete hit a total of only 49 home runs in his career that spanned 14 years. Mickey Mantle, Roger Maris, and All-Stars ignored our pleas for autographs.

We went back home and when the specifics of the game came up in our discussion, we would quickly try to divert the conversation by emphasizing Tom's foresight in getting us into the park early and the "experience" of it all.

The ledges of the walls at that time were flat. They were not peaked to a point and there were no baskets installed underneath until late in the 1969 season. The bleacher fans had begun hopping over the wall onto the field, to celebrate the Cubs newfound success.

One day Tom and we took our father to the game. He was a little hung over from the previous night of partying. With the sun shining upon him, with his arms crossed, he rested his head on the right field wall and fell asleep. Stan Musial hit a home run that bounced on the wall directly in front of him, barely missing his head. It seemed too funny and cool then, sort of scary now.

From the front row, we were able to yell down to the ground crew. We knew most of them from our years working with the Bears. One member of the crew would bring the wooden batter's box frame filled with chalk from the area beneath the right field bleachers. Ron Santo was in a terrible slump. Taking a cue from our Uncle Tom, who had us relay suggestions to Roosevelt Taylor, we had that member of the ground crew deliver a note to

Ron, suggesting that he move closer to the plate. From our spot in the bleachers we watched as the note was delivered.

Ron went on a hitting tear. In a radio interview he told Vince Lloyd that he moved closer to the plate. What a moment! Years later, we would occasionally see Ron at Joe Pepitone's night club. Ron told us he remembered getting the note and the result. We did not drink alcohol, ordering only Coca Cola. Our nickname at the club was the "Cokeheads" as we did a lot of "coke'n and joke'n".

We remember one game in 1963, when racing home after school to see the last few innings, we were able to see Cubs relief pitcher Lindy McDaniel enter the game against the Giants with two outs and the score tied. He proceeded to pick off Willie Mays at second base for the third out, and then leading off the Cubs half of the inning, he hit a walk off home run to win the game.

On another school day, our friend Gary Jowers had been sent to the principal's office for bad behavior. A while later, he entered our class and told our teacher that he had an important message to tell the twins. The teacher gave him permission to deliver the message. As he got near our desks, he whispered, "The Cubs are winning 3 to 1." What fun!

In the summer of 1964, we read that the famed Yankees were staying at the Bismarck Hotel while playing the White Sox at old Comiskey Park. With pen and paper in hand, we boys took the "L" downtown hunting for autographs. Surely, Mickey Mantle and Roger Maris could not ignore us like at the All-Star Game. Our treasure trove of signatures procured that day include Mickey, Roger, Yogi Berra, Elston Howard, Moose Skowron, Whitey Ford, Mel Stottlemeyer, Jim Bouton, Phil Rizzuto, Mel Allen, and others. This was amazing!

We had a gift for "sniffing out" players when not in uniform or their usual habitat. We are reminded of trying to get Jerry Kramer's autograph when we were kids. Jerry was a guard for the

Green Bay Packers, who became a member of the Pro Football Hall of Fame and is most remembered for the block that enabled Bart Starr to score the winning touchdown in the "Ice Bowl", the 1967 NFL Championship game. Jerry was in his street clothes, watching a Cubs game at Wrigley. We were the only two people in the ballpark to recognize him. Kramer refused to sign, "Ahh, Come on!"

As we revisit some of the autographs collected, we are reminded of axiom learned with our collecting baseball cards. The value lies not in the monetary value of the collection, but rather in the memories we have of obtaining them.

Once we entered high school, we no longer collected autographs. Gone were the days when we did not start our trip home via the "L" until there was next to no life surrounding the immediate area around Wrigley Field. We would often go with our friend Pat Gage, who was a grade school classmate. He had a car, so often we would travel to the park in his automobile. Was adulthood upon us? Perhaps, but maturity was trailing!

In our senior year at Morton East, we convinced the teachers of the two honors math classes that the two classes should compete in a softball championship. This was fantastic. One class hour was taken up by Rich Kraig and us securing an official clincher softball at the local sporting goods store. Another hour was taken up by going out to chalk up the foul lines and secure the bases This was followed by an hour for the game.

We convinced the powers to be to include the championship in the annual awards day assembly. We made a trophy which was presented to us as part of the program. The other 3,000 students had no idea what was taking place.

We also participated in another type of sport. Along with fellow honors math and science students Rich Kraig, Lonnie Sacchi, Jim Sebek and Mario Calderone, we started having regular outings to the two Chicago burlesque establishments. Sometimes we were joined by George Zemaitis, Glen Ferrentino and Bill

Darr. One evening a group of boys from New Trier High School were also in the audience.

The "Follies Theater" was on State Street and Van Buren Ave. This area is now the location of the Harold Washington Library.

The "Rialto Theater" was just down the block around Jackson Boulevard.

Entry to the theaters went something like this, "Are you over 18?", "No." "Do you have the $2.00 to get in?", "Yes"!

The performers were at best second tier and featured the French love capsule, Miss "Penny Cillin"; the sex computer in motion, Miss "Uni Vac;" and direct from Japan, Miss "Socka To Me". We all put our hands together to welcome Miss "I Need A Man". The audience was entertained by the comedy team of Scurvy Miller and his straight man, Bob Lee. Lest we forget, we were able to buy "The Wonder Book" for those 18 to 80, sold by "Sunshine".

We discovered that if Sunshine lost his place while doing his sales pitch, he would have to start over from the beginning. He resorted to delivering his pitch in lightning speed, less we interrupt him. The "Wonder Book" was, in fact, a book on etiquette written in 1902. Purchasers were too embarrassed to admit they had been defrauded.

We bought one book. In our honor's chemistry class, Mario Calderone gave a terrific impression of Sunshine's presentation. Little did Mario know that the teacher was behind him, watching over his shoulder. "Let me see the book", the teacher said. Without missing a beat, Mario asked, "Are you over 18?"

We went for the hilarity that ensued, not necessarily for the hope of seeing naked women. As a result of our laughter, we had side aches that equaled those experiences with our first workout with Coach Hudgens.

True to form, we all stayed afterwards to get autographs of the various stars (?)!

Unlike our classmates, we discussed these experiences with

our parents. They talked about the era of true burlesque. We really were not that interested.

In honor's math class, our teacher would assign homework problems to be solved with solutions presented on the blackboard the next time the class met. We students were instructed to write our names and the numbers of the problems we felt confident that we could solve on a piece of paper. The folded papers were placed in a hat and the teacher would draw from the hat to determine who was going to solve the problem on the blackboard.

Problem #14 was impossible to solve. None of us knew the answer. Yet, when determining who was going to solve it on the blackboard, the teacher unfolded a paper and said, "Rich Kraig, number 14!" Rich was incredulous, stating "I didn't write down 14, that is not my handwriting!"

The teacher was not amused and set out to uncover the mystery! This event happened on the last day before Christmas vacation.

In the first class held upon returning from vacation, our teacher said, "I have spent the ENTIRE vacation analyzing who could be the perpetrator of this CRIME. I have narrowed it down to two SUSPECTS, Mario Calderone or Jim Sebek". The smartest of all students in the class, both were the only students to close the top like a tent when writing the number 4.

The perpetrator was Jim Sebek, our school's only National Merit Scholar. Jim had rather large ears that turned crimson red when holding in laughter. Our teacher noticed and asked, "What's so funny James?" All of us students could not contain ourselves and the entire classroom burst into laughter!

We could not believe that this prank had been blown up so out of proportion! Solving the mystery became our teacher's obsession! He proclaimed, "You are not college material!"

To summarize: We wasted class time on a softball game, we attended the local burlesque theaters, and the school's only merit scholar assigned an unsolvable question to an unsuspecting classmate. Maybe our teacher had a point!

We took our SAT exam on a Saturday. The night before, the "honors" group went to a concert at the Arie Crown Theater in McCormick Place. The concert remains one of the best we ever attended. Featured acts included Peter and Gordon, the Hollies, the Buckinghams, and the Shadows of Knight. We all sang along to "I go to Pieces", "World Without Love", "Look through Any Window", "Bus Stop", "Kind of a Drag", "Don't you Care" and "Gloria", that is G L O R I A!.

Perhaps this resulted in our very good, but not great, scores. The test can now be taken multiple times. We were not aware of this option and are not sure the option existed at that time.

Once we turned 16 and started working in the summer, we were not able to go to as many games. We went mostly on weekends. This held true through our years at Yale.

Our summer jobs were at our father's place of employment, Hayes Lochner, Inc. Typographers. Carl was first a messenger, and later assisted in the shipping department and the office. Tony became quite skilled as a proof press operator. The other operators were at least ten years older than the two of us.

One proof press operator, Eddie Shimon was a rabid Cubs fan. He would hide behind his press and sneak a listen to the Cubs games on his pocket transistor radio. One game ended with Don Kessinger being called out home plate. Eddie was extremely angry. "He was safe by five feet!" We reminded him that he was listening to, not watching the game. Such enjoyment!

On another occasion, Eddie and another press operator, Gino Allesandri, decided to leave work early and go to the Arlington Park RaceTrack. They developed a fool proof plan. Gino was to inform the foreman that he had a doctor's appointment. Eddie was to feign being sick. After licking his hands to make them moist and dabbing his forehead with hot water, Eddie told the foreman of his illness. The foreman did not buy into the plan and refused Eddie permission to go home. Eddie was furious!

"A guy could be dying, and they still won't let you go home", Eddie proclaimed! We informed him that he wasn't really sick. Eddie responded that "It's the principle of the thing"!

On Opening Day in 1969, our brother Tom feigned sickness to be excused from his teaching job at a Cicero grade school. Rushing to the bleachers, he ran into Eddie Shimon!

The Cubs won the game with a walk off home run by Willie Smith. Tom called us that night at Yale and held the phone close to his TV so we could hear the replay of Jack Brickhouse hysterically, but excitedly describe the action! "Hey! Hey! Way to go Willie!"

One day, Gino received a letter from Italy. He did not speak or read Italian. The company janitor, Gus LoPresti was proficient in Italian, but was finishing up his vacation. We filled Gino's head with visions of grandeur. He inherited great wealth! He was royalty! We called him "Count Allesandri".

Gus returned to work and read the letter. Gino's hopes sunk like a lead balloon. A distant relative in Italy was asking Gino for money!

During the summers before our junior and senior years at Yale, Tony worked the night shift. He started work at 8 pm and finished at 3:30 am. "Lunch" was from midnight to 12:30. At that time a bridge went over Illinois Street at Michigan Ave. Tony would sit on the small stoop separating the wall of the bridge from the sidewalk. Mom would always make a sandwich for Tony to take to work.

Tony befriended a homeless man, Bill, and most days shared his sandwich with him. One night, Bill asked Tony, "Do you think you could ask your Mom to make something other than a minced ham sandwich?".

Tony was often approached by ladies of the evening who asked if he was interested in a "date". Somehow, Tony's offer of a minced ham sandwich was not enough to secure the ladies' company.

Tony's job as a proof press operator was to run a proof of the job set by hand with type from an old California job case. The type was old. There were scratches on many of the letters, open o's, uncrossed t's, etc. To fill in the missing pieces, ink was often added to the press. Unfortunately, this often made the letters blurry when looked at closely. The proofs were to be made camera ready so that a plate could be made for reproducing the advertisement. A densitometer was purchased to measure the density of the ink. Through trial and error an acceptable range on the densitometer was established. A test bar was run at the bottom of the job to make sure the proper amount of ink was added to the press.

There was one African American employee at Hayes Lochner, Robert "Brother" Meekins, the janitor. Tony asked Brother Meekins to join him in an experiment. Tony and Brother Meekins each measured their skin using the densitometer. The difference was inconsequential. Tony replied that there were years of discrimination for a meaningless difference in skin color, particularly since half the year he was trying for as dark a suntan as possible. This is something we will always remember.

While acquiring our MBA's at the University of Chicago, we were able to go to many games. Classes were usually over by noon and we also took some of our classes in their night program offered in the University' downtown branch located on Delaware St, across from the John Hancock building.

Each night of class we would walk past the Westin Hotel. We would always have great, albeit short, discussions with the doorman, Lorenzo White. He was a wonderful, kind black gentleman. In 2009, the Chicago Tribune featured him in an article entitled "Veteran Doorman puts a friendly face on the Westin". The article stated that he was 73 years old, so we first began our conversations when he was 38!

Periodically we would continue to see and talk to him throughout the years. True to our practical nature as described with Eric Segal driving us to campus at Yale, Lorenzo often watched our cars for us, saving us the expense and hassle of paying in nearby parking garages!

Just as in high school, we studied at our kitchen table, while watching the original 38 episodes of "The Honeymooners" and "The Tonight Show" starring Johnny Carson. A Canadian production, "Night Heat", was also a favorite.

We would often have a pizza delivered. If the pizza had not arrived by 10:00, our Mom would become angry. "Aren't you guys going to order a pizza tonight?"

As we went to so many games, we befriended many of the right field bleacher "regulars", all seasoned retirees. Carl Leone was about a 70 years old Italian, John the "Swede" of that nationality was of similar age, as was Brother Williams an affable man of color. The sage of the bleachers was Caleb "Chet" Chestnut. Chet was proud black gentleman around 80 years old. He had been going to Cubs games since Wrigley Field first opened. He had a wooden leg, was heavy set, and used a cane when walking.

As they pretty much sat in the top row, we moved up to sit with them. We were joined by Mickey Hornick, a good friend who we met in the bleachers. Sometimes Bruce Levine and George Castle would join us. Bruce is the baseball expert for Chicago's most popular sports radio station "Score 670AM" and George went on to write numerous books about the Cubs.

We learned that Carl Leone's daughter worked for JAM Productions, which at that time, booked all rock and roll gigs. Carl would tell us of having the Beatles over for dinner and that his daughter dated Rick Huxley of the Dave Clark Five. We all sang their songs, just as we had done in high school. As the Cubs were prepared to take the field to start the game, he would stand up and yell "Let em loose"!

John the "Swede" would never talk but would listen intently

to the discussions. One day in 1972 the discussion turned to Randy Hundley, who had just returned to the Cubs. The consensus was, "He can't do anything anymore; he can't run, he can't hit, he can't throw." Silent John, broke his silence adding, "can't f _ _ _!" We could not believe it!

In 1972, soon after Leo Durocher was fired and replaced by Whitey Lockman, one conversation went as follows: "You watch Burt Hooton, he is really going to start pitching well. He suffered negatively because of Durocher's tough love. It will be different with the more mild, supportive Whitey Lockman." Chet listened, paused for a while, then stated: "You can give a dog dogfood, or you can give it steak, but it's still a dog!"

On the first day of our marketing class at business school, the professor handed out a list of 300 multiple choice questions, stating that 100 of these were to be the final exam. We could work on the questions' answers independently or in groups. We arrived at our answers and set out to commit them to memory.

We would bring the list of questions to the ballpark and Chet would quiz us. If we answered correctly, Chet would immediately go onto the next question. If we gave an incorrect answer, Chet would respond, "sure you want to stay with that answer?"

Chet died in the late seventies. We had visited him in the hospital. We, our parents, and Mickey Hornick attended the services at a funeral home on Indiana Avenue on Chicago's southside. The next day we were pallbearers. It was an extremely hot, humid day in August. When the casket was sliding off the hearse, our knees buckled momentarily. Afterwards, Brother Williams, also a pallbearer, told us that when serving in this function, us little guys should always grab the middle of the rail. We responded that we hoped it would not become a regular occurrence.

One game in 1972 against the Pittsburgh Pirates stands out in our memory. In the Cubs half of an inning, Jose Cardenal hit a line drive to right center field, and took a wide turn around first base, threatening to go to second. Roberto Clemente threw on the line to first base, nearly nailing Jose as he scampered back to first base. In the very next inning, Roberto Clemente hit a ball to the exact same area. He also took a wide turn towards second base. Jose Cardenal threw on the line to first base trying to nab Clemente. Seeing this, Roberto proceeded leisurely to second base. The difference between a good player and a Hall of Famer!

That winter Clemente died in a plane crash while bringing first aid supplies to Nicaragua. In a game we attended the following season against the Pirates, a Puerto Rican gentleman stood at attention holding a picture of Clemente draped in black. For some reason, Ronnie "Woo Woo" Wickers, famed Chicago Cubs fan and bleacher member, and the gentleman got into a serious scuffle. Our friend Mickey Hornick excitedly proclaimed, "This is the greatest game I've ever been to!"

June 29, 1973, the Cubs Gene Hiser hit a home run with two outs in the 9th inning against Met's pitcher Buzz Capra to tie the game 3 to 3. The Cubs won the game in extra innings. It was the only home run Gene hit in his major league career. Maybe God was a Cubs fan after all.

Joe Mantegna, the actor, sat in the right center field bleachers. Later he wrote a popular play about his experiences entitled "The Bleacher Bums". Joe also went to our high school. He could never shake the reputation of being the third most avid Cubs fan at Morton East. Sorry Joe!

OUR CUBS EXPERIENCE DEEPENS

WHILE WORKING AS A STAFF or senior staff member for Price Waterhouse, Carl's love for the Cubs helped him secure a plum assignment. He worked on audits of the Cubs (The Chicago National League Ball Club) from 1973 through 1975. At that time, the Cubs were owned by Philip Knight (P.K.) Wrigley, of the William Wrigley chewing gum family. Mr. Wrigley had inherited the Cubs and the gum company from his father William Wrigley, Jr.

This experience helped shape our future journey with the Cubs. It is at this time, that through Carl, we made lifetime friendships with Jerry and June Foran. Jerry was first controller for the Cubs and June an accountant for the team.

Carl would very rarely see Yosh Kawano, the Cubs clubhouse manager we saw our first day of work with the Bears in 1963. Yosh was famous for not going up to the Cubs office. His domain was the clubhouse.

P.K. Wrigley was famous for being a recluse. He was rarely seen at the ballpark bearing his family name and most of the Cubs front office personnel had never met him. He was one of the wealthiest people in the world. He considered the Cubs to be a hobby and ran it as such.

Jack Brickhouse and others advertised, "come spend a pic-

nic in the sun", plan your getaway at beautiful Wrigley Field.",
etc. 25,000 unreserved seats went on sale the morning of each
game. The attendance for these years was 1,351,705 in 1973;
1,015,378 in 1974; and 1,034,819 in 1975.

The attendance in our younger years ranged from about
600,000 to 980,000. Attendance first broke one million in
1968. Tony's children and our nieces and nephews were amazed
as to how many balls we caught in the bleachers as youths. We
competed with very few fans for a prized ball hit into the stands!
We remember one day when a ball sailed into the bleachers and
we were fighting for the ball, trying to pull our competitors' arms
and hands apart. We looked up to realize that we were competing with one another.

The Cubs' offices were at Wrigley Field in an area roughly
behind home plate. You had to wind your way around a circular staircase to arrive to the offices on the second floor. The
organization's year end was October 31st, and there were strict
reporting deadlines to send in Form 10Q to the SEC (Securities
and Exchange Commission). As a result, us Price Waterhouse
staff members would work overtime at the park. We were given
our own key so we could arrive early, but mostly stay late. A few
times, Carl's superior Mike Bryniarski and he would don uniform tops found in one of the offices while completing our work.

The Price Waterhouse staff used the conference room as
its work area. The room had adjoining doors to the offices of
general manager John Holland on one side and that of Blake
Cullen, assistant general manager, on the other. With their doors
open, and trade winds blowing, Carl would stop hitting keys of
the calculator, to better hear these officials discussing a possible
transaction. Once he heard of a trade of Glenn Beckert to the
San Diego Padres for Jerry Morales. He hurriedly excused himself to call Tony at his Arthur Young & Company office with
news of the trade.

A treasured friend, Mary Dease, shares our birthday of May

22. Mary served as Mr. Holland's executive secretary. She later served as administrative assistant to the chairman of Winston & Strawn, former U.S. Attorney Dan Webb.

Later John Cox became assistant general manager to E.R. "Salty" Saltwell. John is currently a scout with the San Francisco Giants. He previously scouted for the New York Yankees. He specialized in scouting baseball players from the "Pacific Rim". During his time with the Yankees, John was involved in the signings of such notable players as Hideki Matsui, Chin-Ming Wang and Jose Contreras.

While with the Cubs, we joined him in his scouting box. Looking over his shoulder as he wrote notes, we noticed that he wrote down that a Cubs player had shown great hustle going after a foul ball. Unfortunately, that foul ball was a grounder that had first hit off the third base wall. Evidently, his scouting improved over the years.

Until the advent of free agency which requires that salaries be published, player salaries were kept under lock and key at the Price Waterhouse office. Carl would memorize them and share them with Tony. We remember one time when we went to a Blackhawks game with Mike Bryniarski and the audit manager, Doug Calvin. Tony blurted out, "I can't believe the Cubs are paying Carmen Fanzone $_____." Luckily, Carl did not get into trouble.

It is now public information that the largest salaries were to Ernie Banks, Ron Santo and Billy Williams and approximated $100,000. Ferguson Jenkin's salary was not far behind.

A Price Waterhouse audit procedure step was to test the Cubs ticket revenue. This was before the arrival of computers and electronic tickets. The procedure uncovered a box office shortage. Cubs personnel were in a dizzy. They decided to bring this matter up with P.K. Wrigley personally. As this was a rare chance to personally meet Mr. Wrigley, Price Waterhouse's audit manager and partner made sure they attended.

The shortage was predicted to be about $16,000. When Carl and others were ushered into Mr. Wrigley's 16th floor office in the Wrigley Building, Mr. Wrigley was on the phone discussing the sale of the Wrigley family's privately owned Catalina Island, off the coast from Los Angeles. In 1975, P.K. deeded over 42,000 acres to the Catalina Island Conservancy. Its' value approximated $600 million. Talk about feeling small!

Mr. Wrigley asked as to the purpose of the meeting. After introductions by Cubs office executives, Mike Bryniarski explained the situation. Carl thought Mike was rambling and missing key points and took his turn to clarify the situation. When Carl finished, Mr. Wrigley spoke next, "I don't know what the hell you guys are talking about". So much for clarity!

Carl was asked by management if he wanted to come to work for the Cubs. His response was that he was only interested in being the Cubs field manager or general manager. Little did we know that a generation later, a Yale graduate with baseball knowledge would propel to fame. Theo Epstein brought championships to the Red Sox and the Cubs. We do know that the Bears won the championship in our **first** year.

In the opening of the 1974 season at Wrigley Field, Carl realized that the Cubs would hold a workout the day prior to the opener. Feigning a doctor's appointment, he called in sick at Price Waterhouse, but really ventured to Wrigley. Carl and Jerry ventured out to the field and had a humorous discussion. To his chagrin, the nightly news was covering the workout, and Carl and Jerry were seen prominently in the background, laughing, and waving their arms. Oops!

The ticket takers for the Cubs belonged to a union. They worked other venues besides the ballpark. These individuals were a terrific source to secure excellent seats. We were able to get front row seats for the 1973 concert at the Arie Crown Theatre featuring Frankie Valli and the Four Seasons. Singing loudly and proudly, like our Mom in our second grade Christmas show,

Frankie Valli gave us the microphone to finish "Rag Doll". We kept the microphone to start the next song, "Sherry". Frankie reached down to secure the microphone, reminding us, "This is my gig". We were excited! "Oh, what a night!"

As a result of that meeting, Jerry Foran became ticket manager and June followed him down to the ticket office.

In 1976, Carl left Price Waterhouse to start Ruzicka & Associates. Jerry asked if we would be interested in season tickets. He assured us that we would get seats near the Chicago Cubs dugout. The price of a box seat ticket was then $4.50. In 1976 there were only 2200 total season tickets sold.

Our full season ticket plan cost $1,458 for four seats. In 2018, this price was $52,869. This historical increase in the price of the tickets makes the increase in Yale's tuition seem modest!

We eventually had four seats in the third row behind the Cubs dugout. This location was a tremendous advantage point to watch the game.

Cubs ticket envelope

Jerry also asked us if we would be interested in having Ruzicka & Associates, sponsor the envelopes used to give tickets to the fans. Our cost would be the artwork and the printing of the envelopes. We thought this would really be a gold mine of new business for our newly established accounting practice.

Calls flooded in. "I can't make it to the 5/21 game, can I exchange it for 5/22?", "My neighbor is sick and can't make it on the 6/7 game, can you help?", "We are coming to game from Elgin, how do we get to the ballpark?", "Is there parking at Wrigley?", "How do you get to the park using public transportation", "Is there a double header on 7/10?"

Being ever- obedient fans, instead of giving out the Cubs' phone number, we did our best to help!

After starting our accounting firm, Jerry Foran would call us occasionally to tell us a recent story or to ask us advice.

One story remembered involved a reserve outfielder in the mid 70's. Salaries paled in comparison to those today. Direct deposit did not exist. It was common practice for some players to cash their paycheck in the concession office. The outfielder was on the disabled list, so rather than his usual practice of picking up the check in person and cashing it, the check was mailed. Jerry received a call from the outfielder's wife, "The Cubs must have made some kind of mistake with my husband's check." Jerry asked why. She answered, "the amount my husband brings home is usually around $2,000, and this check is for $2,500."

At that time certain passive investment income and losses had no limitations. Various oil and gas tax shelters were prevalent. One day June called our office asking to compute a paycheck utilizing 100 exemptions!

Andy McPhail, now president of the Philadelphia Phillies, got his start as an intern with the Cubs. One day when visiting the Forans at their Cubs office, we told Andy about our ideas on some sort of tax imposed on wealthier teams or a revenue sharing agreement to help promote league balance. We were applying the diversity lessons which helped get us into Yale!

In 1981, the Cubs opened the season losing 13 of its first 14 games. Jerry Foran thought it would be a good idea to start fresh with a second opening day. A stroke of genius. The Cubs won game #15.

Because we were fixtures at the ballpark, we were permitted to go inside before the gates opened for business. We would go through the "blue door" alongside Clark St. Inside, the desk was manned by Howie Roberts. Howie, now retired, was a famous sportswriter for the Chicago Daily News and then the Chicago Tribune.

One day when hurrying to get his ticket validated by Howie, Carl unintentionally walked past one of that day's umpires, Terry Tata, who was in the middle of transacting business of his own. Terry got real upset and "kicked Carl out of the game!". Carl called Jerry Foran and was told not to worry about it, the umpires had no jurisdiction." Phew"!

When the Wrigley family sold the Cubs to the Chicago Tribune in 1981 (for $20.5 million), Jerry and June retained their positions for a while, but were eventually fired. After working for the Chicago Blitz of the USFL (United States Football League) until the disbandment of the league, Jerry and June eventually moved to work for the Buffalo Bills Football team. Jerry became Vice President of Finance and June became Director of Ticket Services.

During the O.J. Simpson murder trial, one famed exchange concerned imprints of Bruno Magli shoes purportedly worn by O.J. while committing the murder. His famous response was, "I would never wear such bad ass shoes." O.J. was acquitted. Later for the civil trial, Jerry uncovered a picture of O.J. wearing the shoes at a Bills game that honored past players. Simpson was found guilty.

In the murder trial, one of Simpson's "Dream Team" lawyers was our Yale classmate, Barry Scheck. Barry later became director of the "Innocence Project", an organization committed to exonerating wrongly convicted people through DNA testing. At our 25th Yale Reunion in 1996, Barry had a hard time matching our steps on the dance floor. We told him it was in our "DNA"!

In 1988 the Bills won their first of 4 consecutive, league championships. As a souvenir of this accomplishment Jerry and June sent us napkin holders that were replicas of the team's championship ring.

In 1989, at one of the Cubs vs Giant divisional series games, Carl went to the game with Terry Hrabak, our childhood friend of no hitter fame, and our father. Carl brought along the ring to show Terry. Steve Stone, former major league pitcher and broadcaster of the Cubs that year happened to be sitting alongside Carl. Steve won the American League Cy Young award as the league's best pitcher in 1980. His record was 25-7 for the Baltimore Orioles.

It so happened that Steve was proudly wearing the ring given to him by the Orioles commemorating his accomplishment. On more than a few occasions Steve was asked to show his ring to his fans. The baseball bases were denoted with diamonds and the record engraved on its face.

After one showing, Carl told Steve, "You know Steve, that ring is great, but my childhood friend next to me, Terry Hrabak once pitched a slow pitch, rubber ball, two man on a side no hitter." Carl reached into his pocket and quickly showed Steve the napkin holder replica ring. Steve left his seat shortly thereafter, never to return. Steve is now a current TV announcer for the White Sox.

Cubs fans versus Sox fans is a disagreement the continues to this day.

Tony was on the board of directors of Special Children's Charities. He and Anne were to sit with Billy Pierce, famous former White Sox pitcher, at the Charities" annual gala. On the way to the event Tony gave Anne the Franklin Baseball Encyclopedia section on Billy Pierce and asked her to memorize as much information about Billy's career as she could and then periodically drop facts into the dinner conversation. Anne was terrific. She would suddenly state to Billy that she could not believe he was traded for Aaron Robinson. Later she stated how fantastic Billy was in 1955 when his earned run average was 1.97. Billy could not believe that Anne knew so much about him!

Carl told Billy about an incident around 1959. We were playing catch in our backyard. Our father was working and admonished us to stop as we might break a window. Our Uncle Bill was watching. Carl tried to replicate the wind up of the Sox star and proclaimed, "Look Uncle Bill, Billy Pierce". The ball went right throw a window! To quote Jack Brickhouse, "Oh Boy"!

Howard Pizer, Senior Executive Vice President of the Chicago White Sox, also served on the board of Special Children's Charities. Howard asked Tony what he would do to revive the Sox franchise. Unlike his answer to Wally Phillips, this time Tony gave a serious response. He proposed a return to free television. The Sox, under the direction of co-owners Eddie Einhorn and Jerry Reinsdorf, were the first Chicago sports franchise to broadcast on pay tv: a new regional cable television network, "SportsVision". The move was a financial disaster, particularly because the Cubs games were still being televised on free tv via WGN. Tony also suggested that the Sox return to their classic black and white uniform with the classic Sox in white on their black hat and a black SOX on the white jersey.

After, the Cubs won the 2016 World series, Tony bumped into Rick Hahn, Chicago White Sox general manager, in downtown Glencoe. Tony introduced himself and suggested to Rick to not be afraid to go young.

Tony had the good fortune of meeting President Barack Obama before Barack was famous. Barack was chairman of the board of a client, Chicago Annenberg Challenge. Later we became auditors of CURE (Citizens United for Research in Epilepsy). On his first visit to CURES's office Tony noticed framed frontpage newspaper stories about local elections. He learned that CURE was founded by Susan Axelrod whose daughter is epileptic. Susan's husband is David Axelrod. David was the chief strategist for President Obamas presidential campaign. CURE officed with David and had three employees at the time who were all Sox fans.

Tony and the staff would engage in friendly Cubs vs. Sox banter. One day President Obama came to the office for a meeting with David and the campaign team. Barack lived in Hyde Park and had a southside allegiance to the Sox. Tony told him that hopefully the United States was to have its first African American President. Perhaps it was also time for Cubs fans and Sox fans to peacefully co-exist and support each team. In the few games when the teams played each other Tony could root for the Cubs and Barack for the Sox. Other than those games we should pull for each other. Afterall, both teams are from Chicago. Tony ultimately commented that he could get there intellectually, but not emotionally. Barack agreed.

In the first row, with a single ticket, sat Tommy Donnellan:

Tommy had both mental and physical challenges. He loved the Cubs. Every game he would take an eight miles bus ride down Addison Street from his home that he shared with his elderly mother. He proudly wore a walkie talkie receiver on his belt. Tommy was about 5'5" and weighed around 250 pounds. His speech was difficult to understand as he had no teeth. We came to know and love him. We could probably fill up a book with stories about him and our friendship. We choose a few:

Tommy would always ask us to buy him a coke and hot dog. Many times, we barely had enough money to buy these items for ourselves. When we had little money to spare, we would try not to make eye contact with him, as we knew the result would be us reaching for our wallets. To ignore Tommy during the game was a difficult task. Letting our guard down, we caught his glance, "Tommy is feeling kind of dry"! "Ok Tommy we'll get you a coke". We joked that we had developed a reflex reaction. If

Tommy turned around to see us, we would automatically reach for our wallets! One opening day we brought him a six - foot long submarine sandwich!

We learned that Tommy's walkie talkie came from a friend at Uniden, a company specializing in electronic equipment. At a game, Tommy asked us if he could have our tickets for an upcoming game and we obliged. The next time we saw him he was proudly wearing a new receiver. He had used our tickets as barter!

Tommy also had season tickets to the Chicago Bears. One September Saturday game, a worried Tommy told us, "Tommy have terrible problem". Concerned we asked him what the problem was. He responded, "Tomorrow Cubs and Bears play same day". Such a dilemma!

One Cubs game in September1988, President Reagan threw out the first pitch. We were at work in our office when we received a call from Tommy. We had never experienced him being so excited. We could almost feel the saliva through the receiver, "Tommy see Reagan, Tommy see Reagan, Tommy see so many G men, Tommy see so many G men!" There was a ticket seller at the park named Larry Regan who knew Tommy. We feigned ignorance, "So what, you see Larry Regan all the time, no big deal?". "No, president, president", proclaimed Tommy!

We would carry on long conversations with him. Just as with Essel and Spaniel back in Yale's dining hall, this amazed fellow fans around us as they could not understand a word he said.

This is somewhat perplexing, as Carl has no idea what his wife is saying when using her native Cantonese language or the Chinese official language of Mandarin! The southern drawl of Anne's relatives from Kentucky and Alabama also presents some challenges!

Tommy became a fixture at most of our family events including races, office gatherings, and holidays. We employed him as a messenger. A fifteen minutes trip was about an hour for Tommy.

He was too busy charming our clients! Once Herb Lindsay won a road race in Rosemont and did not want to lug home the trophy. We rolled a small piece of paper under the arm of the figurine runner and presented the trophy to Tommy for being "Messenger of the Year"!

Later Tommy's mother died. He continued to live alone in the family home, with Carl acting as unofficial guardian. He also became a ticket holder for the Bulls and the DePaul Blue Demons basketball teams.

Tommy's doctor had told him that he must lose a lot of weight. It was difficult to control him. In many arguments we would tell him of the importance of shedding some pounds. In the middle of our exasperation, Tommy deftly changed the subject, "Michael Jordon a pretty good player?" We could almost see the rolodex flipping over in Tommy's brain as he tried to come up with the proper diverting retort.

With the respect to bartering and changing the subject, Tommy was brilliant!

Tommy died after getting hit by a car in 1991. Fittingly he was on his way to a DePaul Lady Blue Demon basketball game. He was laid out with his Cubs jacket given to him by the Cubs groundcrew. To honor Tommy and provide a fifth seat, we added his front row seat to our season ticket package.

Carl, Tommy Donnellan, Tony

Celebrities often sat near us. One game Tom Selleck, television star of "Magnum, P.I." and now "Blue Bloods", sat in front of us, taking notes for his upcoming move, "Mr. Baseball". Tony asked him for his autograph to give to his daughters. Somewhat reluctantly, Tom obliged, but claimed Tony's pen did not work. Tony replied, "Because it's a pencil"!

Another game Billy Corgan of the Smashing Pumpkins sat nearby. We asked him if he was looking for lead singers.

Other games and incidents stay in our memory:

Tony took our nephew Mike to his first game in 1972. At 2 ½ years of age they sat through an entire extra inning game. Mike did not want to go home.

For a few years, our brother Tom and his two sons had season tickets on the first base side of home plate. When Dave Kingman would come to bat, we would all stand and motion towards left field, reminiscent of Babe Ruth pointing where is home run would land in the 1932 World Series.

Our sister and her family visited Chicago in the summer of 1975. Along with our brother Tom's son Mike {age 6), we took Barb's children Kathe (age 9), Deb (age 7) and Dave (age 4) to the Cubs game. First, we went on a Wendella boat ride along the Chicago River and visited the Lincoln Park Zoo. After the game, we played in the playground near the 31st Street Beach along the Lakefront. The day's excursion started around 9:00 in the morning and ended around 7:00 in the evening.

Upon arriving home, Kathe seemed forlorn. Our Mom asked her what was wrong. Kathe replied, "There is nothing to do!"

Tony's daughter Carrie was born on May 7, 1977. She became quite the fan at an early age. Her favorite player was Dave Kingman. In 1979 Dave hit 48 homeruns and hit 18 in limited duty in 1980. In 1981 he was traded to the New York Mets.

At the beginning of the 1981 season Tony asked Carrie if she was excited about the season starting. Carrie, not yet four years old, replied negatively and Tony asked why. Carrie answered that

The Cubs had traded that guy. Which guy Tony asked? "Kingman", she replied.

At the last home game of the 1979 season held September 26, 1979 we were joined by a Yale classmate, Greg Watkins. During the game we were exchanging friendly banter with the 3rd base umpire, Ed Montague. The Cubs were losing the game and in the last inning a Met batter hit a line drive down the 3rd baseline. The ball hit the chalk and Ed started his motion to call the ball fair. We yelled for him to give us a break. He heard us and continued his motion signaling the ball foul. He tipped his cap to us.

Years later we saw Ed in the visitor's clubhouse. He acknowledged doing so. Greg tells the story at his local watering hole. Even now Greg has a hard time believing it.

In that same game right fielder Larry Biittner dove for a sinking line drive. He missed the ball and ran in circles trying to find it so he could throw it back to the infield. The crowd was all helping him, "Larry, it is under your hat." Larry's cap came off when he dove for the ball and the ball rolled into his hat flipping it over thus hiding the ball.

Later we went out to dinner with Yosh and his good friend Prentice Marshall, famous judge of the United States District Court for the Northern District of Illinois. Judge Marshall was a huge Cubs fan and told us the Larry Biittner game was his favorite of all-time.

Sitting directly behind the dugout we became friends with many players. A special relationship was built with Cubs relief pitcher Bill Caudill. When the Cubs pitcher got in trouble, we would stand up and yell "Caudill". Bill would get up and pretend to start warming up in the bullpen. Later a young lady near our seats was celebrating her 16th birthday. We convinced Bill to give her a kiss, a thrill of her young lifetime.

On April 1, 1982 Bill was traded to the New York Yankees. He became agent Scott Boras' first client. We were quite upset.

Our disappointment was made greater when he was to be replaced by Herman Segelke. Herman pitched a grand total of 4.1 innings in 1982.

Tony went to the Friday April 29, 1983 game against the Dodgers. Tony left work early to go to the game and arrived in his business suit. Late in the game, Cubs manager Lee Elia went to the mound to visit the pitcher. Tony was sitting in the first row directly behind the stairs into the dugout. When Elia returned, Tony calmly but sarcastically said "Put Caudill in". The Cubs lost the game 4-3 resulting in a 5-14 start to the season.

On his way home, Carl called wanting to know what happened. Lee Elia had gone on a postgame tirade that was recorded by Les Grobstein. This is a famous part of Cubs lore. In his rant Elia swore consistently and criticized the Cubs fans, stating that "85% of the f'n people have jobs and the other f'n 15% come to the Cubs games".

Tony told Carl what happened. Carl was afraid we would lose our seats and called Jerry Foran. Jerry told him Elia would be gone before we were. He was correct.

At the first playoff game held against the Giants October 1, 1989, Giant pitcher Scott Garrelts broke his bat swinging at a pitch and the top of the bat came like a frisbee directly toward Tony's head. Tony ducked and the bat broke the arm of the lady sitting behind Tony. The incident was shown vividly on the TV. Carl, at home, immediately was flooded with phone calls inquiring about Tony and his family's safety.

Sitting behind the Cubs dugout near 3rd base, we often engaged in friendly conversation with other team third baseman or third base coaches. We have fond memories of Ray Knight of the Reds, Jerry Manuel third base coach for the Mets, Jerry Royster of the Braves, and Bill Fahey of the Giants.

Felipe Alou, former outstanding outfielder, was the third base coach for the Montreal Expos. Felipe had two brothers that also were successful players, Matty and Jesus. Tony yelled out, "Hey

Felipe! Hey Felipe! I know your brother! Manny Mota!". We all had a good chuckle!

Steve Dillard, a Cubs infielder, asked, "How old are you guys?" This reminds us of one of our father's axioms, "Age is just a number!"

Some 20-25 years later, when visiting Yosh Kawano in the visitor's clubhouse, we saw these gentlemen, now in different capacities with different teams. They immediately recognized us and greeted us with warmth and laughter. Once again being a twin had its advantages.

At the 1990 All-Star game held in Wrigley Field, Fahey was a bench coach. Along with our nephew Matt, we cheered loudly and continuously late in the game, asking that Bill coach third base. Roger Craig, Giants manager and National League manager, finally relented. As Fahey entered the 3rd base coaches box, he was met with a standing ovation! "F...A...H...E...Y, spells Fahey."!

At that time, nephew Matt was a self-conscious teenager, who was shy of attention. We remedied that by yelling out as loud as we could "Matt", followed by the faintest voice "Williams". After all, we were merely cheering for the Giant third baseman.

On June 13, 1994 Ryne "Ryno" Sandberg announced his first retirement from baseball. He was off to a terrible start as were the Cubs. On June 1st he hit his 4th and 5th home runs of the season against the Phillies. When returning to the dugout, looking into the stands for acclaim, Anne was face down working on her needle point. We kid her that she is the reason Ryno retired. His retirement announcement was overshadowed by the Nicole Simpson murder.

Our Dad was able to be with us on Cubs opening day in 1994 when Tuffy Rhodes hit three home runs against Dwight "Doc" Gooden of the Mets. Luckily, he also attended the 1996 Cubs opener against San Diego. Our brother Tom came from Colorado to join us. The Cubs won 5-4, as Mark Grace hit a walk off single in the 10th inning. Losing pitcher was Hall of Fame reliever Trevor Hoffman. Tom remains so happy that he was able to share this experience with our Dad.

Another remembrance was the June 8, 2003 game against the Yankees. While attempting to catch a pop up near home plate, pitcher Kerry Wood collided violently with first baseman Hee-seop Choi. Choi laid motionless on the infield grass. The siren of the ambulance from the famed firehouse just across the street on Waveland Ave blared louder and louder. The gates leading into the park were opened and the ambulance made its way onto the field to attend to the concussed first baseman. It was an eerie moment in Cubs history.

OUR CUBS JOURNEY
TAKE ANOTHER TURN

O NE GAME CARL WAS WALKING in the concourse at Wrigley and heard a familiar voice, "Ruzicka!" It was Yosh Kawano. We had met him our first day working for the Bears in 1963. This began a journey that brought us closer to the Cubs.

Yosh is a Chicago Cubs legend. He started following the Cubs as a young boy in Los Angeles where the Cubs trained at another Wrigley Field. This was the ballpark used in the original Home Run Derby TV show. We can still vividly recall the announcer, Mark Scott, informing us that "The ballpark favors neither the lefthanded nor righthanded hitters", "every ball not a homer is considered an out". On any ball not hit fair over the fence, the umpire' yelled, "One Out", etc.

Yosh stowed away on the ferry when the Cubs changed their spring training site to Catalina Island. He began working for the Cubs in 1935 as a spring training batboy, and at Wrigley Field as a visiting clubhouse attendant in 1943. He was friends with Ted Williams and Joe DiMaggio, whom he met as teenagers in the old Pacific Coast League!

Yosh and his family were placed in the Poston War Relocation Center in Arizona, an internment camp for Japanese citizens. He served in the Army in World War II. He told us that one day he was on the inside with rifles pointed at him. The next day he was on the outside with his own rifle.

As he was in the Army, Yosh missed working the 1945 World Series between the Cubs and the Detroit Tigers.

We were touched by the fact that Yosh carried a picture taken when he was a young teenager of him and Gabby Hartnett. Gabby was famous for hitting the "Homer in the Gloamin", a walk off homer with darkness setting in that help secure the Cubs pennant in 1938.

Yosh/Gabby Hartnett

Because of Yosh, we were afforded many privileges and experiences that Cubs fans can only dream about, often spending time in the Cubs and, later, visitor clubhouses.

Carl, Yosh, Carrie, Tony in Cubs dugout

In 1993, Yosh arranged for Carrie to meet her favorite player, Dwight Smith, in the tunnel leading to the dugout. Carrie had her picture taken with Dwight sitting on the team dugout bench.

In the spring of 1994, we visited Yosh in the clubhouse during a game. Tony had to use the bathroom facilities. Cubs pitcher, Turk Wendell, sarcastically asked Tony why he had to come into the clubhouse to relieve himself. Tony replied that Turk had more important things to worry about. Turk's record that year was 0 wins and 1 loss, with an Earned Run Average of 11.93.

Turk also inquired, "Don't you guys ever work?" Tony replied, "Don't you think watching the Cubs qualifies as work?"

On another occasion, Rev. Jessie Jackson and Carl stood side by side using the Cubs clubhouse urinals

When auditing the Donors Forum of Chicago, now Forefront, we befriended their controller, Antionette Wright. Antoinette previously worked for Operation Push, an organization founded by Reverend Jessie Jackson. During the Democratic convention in 1999, Antoinette invited Tony to a luncheon party to be held at Rev. Jackson's home. The party was held in Rev. Jackson's yard. Here Tony met singer Gladys Knight.

Before the barbeque, Rev. Jackson had everyone form a circle and join hands while he said grace. Tony held hands with Rev. Al Sharpton on his left and Marion Berry, mayor of the District of Columbia on his right. A young boy from Cicero had come a long way!

On a later occasion, we ran into the Rev. Jackson in the Wrigley Field concourse. Tony explained that he was past president of the Village of Glencoe and that we had had merged Ruzicka & Associates (a five person firm) into a firm with 55 people, and that the new firm subsequently merged into a firm with 2200 people.

We asked Rev. Jackson to repeat after us: "We used to be.... somebody"!

Later, Antoinette became President and Chief Operating Officer of the DuSable Museum of African American History and the Museum became another Ruzicka & Associates client. Tony recommended that the Museum have an open house the night of the 2008 United States Presidential election as hopefully Barack Obama was to be elected and it would be one of the greatest moments in African American history.

Ms. Wright was hesitant as she did not want to involve the Museum in partisan politics. Tony stated that the Museum could open after the polls were closed, and Ms. Wright agreed. A modest $5 admission fee was charged and a map of the United States with each state's electoral college votes was provided to each attendee. We all watched the election night coverage, tallying the electoral votes. Rather than take the expressway home, Tony decided to take local streets and thrilled in the celebrations he witnessed. "Oh what a night"!

We take great pride in our journey away from the racial bigotry that was one of the few negatives about Cicero.

One time when the Cubs were on the road, we visited Yosh in the clubhouse. This was right after a Fox game of the week played at Wrigley. We noticed Sports Hot Zone scouting reports for all players that had been use by the Fox announcers. The strike zone area was divided into 9 squares. Each square showed a batter's performance for pitches thrown in that area and the pitcher's similar performance. We laughingly told Yosh that we had discovered the Cubs weakness: the "pitched ball"!

Perhaps reaching out to someone older after our Dad's death in 1996, but more than likely excited with reuniting with a Cubs legend, we began spending more and more time with Yosh.

We would go out for dinner often. We reminisced about the Cubs and Bears. He recounted that he once was instructed to put whiskey in George Halas' paper cup before a practice. He was impressed that we remembered so many past Cubs and Bears players. We shared hopes for the current Cubs teams. Yosh remembered the fans yelling to "put the twins in". When discussing our exploits, we would resort to an old baseball axiom, "We were just doing our best to help the ballclub!"

Entering any of the restaurants, Yosh would proclaim, "Make way for the three midgets"! We would reply, "Watch it now, Buddy"!

On May 6, 1998 we gave our tickets to clients and good friends, Steve and Barbara Byer. We turned the game on our office radio and learned that Kerry Wood was striking out almost every Houston Astro batter. In the 1994 movie "The Scout", Steve Nebraska, a fictional Yankee pitcher, struck out every batter in his pitching debut. As the game continued and the number of strikeouts increased, we called Yosh in the clubhouse and told him "the Cubs have their own Steve Nebraska"!

Yosh asked if we wanted to go to dinner after the game. We agreed and drove to Waveland Avenue and waited for him to depart the ballpark. He came into the car holding a McDonalds bag and told us he had something for us. In the bag were 3 game balls. He said he had one for Harry Caray's restaurant, one for team president Andy McPhail, and one for us. We asked him to go get Kerry to date and autograph the ball. We then had Yosh write the following notation, "certified game ball Yosh Kawano".

Steve and Barbara Byer, called and said they left early because nothing was happening!

In 1998, we were thrilled following Sammy Sosa hit his numerous home runs. He certainly brought excitement that we had not experience since 1989. Near the end of 1998 we called Arlene Gill in the Cubs office and asked if Sammy had a foundation. He did. We wrote a check to the Foundation and Yosh arranged for us to give it to him personally in the clubhouse before a game.

Soon thereafter a hurricane struck the Dominican Republic. Sammy, with an assist from Rev. Jessie Jackson, used this experience with us to raise money for hurricane relief. He autographed our scorecards of the September 13, 1998 game when he hit homeruns #61 and #62.

When Sammy Sosa hit a home run, he often took a curtain call and would be photographed when doing so. We knew this. On July 25, 2001, Sammy homered and took his call. We stood with the crowd cheering for him. When he was taking his bow, the Cubs hitter lined a ball to left field. The crowd, other than us twins, turned to follow the ball. We stared straight at Sammy. The picture of the curtain call was in the paper the next day. We were the only two fans looking at Sammy and had our hands in the same clapping position. Our shirts looked the same color in the paper.

On the following Saturday morning, acquaintances of ours at the golf course, said that we were being made fun of on Score AM radio. The sportscasters humorously referred to the "aliens" in the picture. It was hilarious! Our sister was offended. How could they say this about her brothers? We explained to her that is exactly how we looked, as if we dropped from space. We only showed up because the photographer was using an infrared lens.

For a while, our nickname changed from "the twins" to "the aliens".

We would normally sit Carl in seat 7 and Tony in seat 10. One day before the game and before our guests had arrived, Cubs third base coach Wendell Kim asked why we did not sit together. We told him we would show him why the next game. Before that game we showed Wendell the picture. He immediately understood.

On another Sammy Sosa curtain call picture, we were excited that we were clearly featured as was our sister Barbara who was visiting our Mom. We excitedly called her to buy the newspaper and look at the back page photograph. Barb called us with a query: "Why was every other fan standing, while we are sitting down?" Unfortunately, we had to let her know that we were all standing as well!

During the last few weeks of the 1998 season, after the players had left the clubhouse, we went in to help Yosh and his assistants. While waiting for Yosh to complete his chores, shower, and dress for dinner, we played whiffle ball with the assistants. We used gloves found in the player lockers. Being left-handed, Carl used the glove belonging to Brant Brown, a Cubs outfielder. The glove was so stiff. How could he catch anything with it?

On September 23rd, in the 9th inning of a game against the Brewers, Brown was about to catch what would have been the game ending third out. Unfortunately, he dropped the ball, three runs came around to score, and the Cubs lost the game. Part of Cubs lore is the radio description of the play. Pat Hughes, play by play announcer, screams "Brant Brown drops the ball! He drops the ball!" This was followed by Ron Santo, color commentator, yelling, "Oh No! Oh No!". This was game 159. Luckily, the Cubs made it to the playoffs

After the Cubs beat the Giants in the tie-breaker game September 28, 1998, Yosh invited us into the clubhouse and celebrate with the players. We did, not leaving for home until 4 in the morning! This was an experience not shared by any other fans. That and many other experiences served as a reminder to not be in such a hurry to grow up! We snapped towels, poured champagne over players' heads, and sang along with the players.

It was reminiscent of the Bears 1963 celebration. We are reminded of another one of our father's axioms, "Don't get old. There is no future in it!"

At a few Cubs games early in the season, we did not dress properly. The weather changes quickly and it can get really cold at Wrigley. Being ever so resourceful and practical, we would call Yosh in the clubhouse and he would provide us with extra player parkas.

Yosh often told the story of Hillary Clinton having to instruct ballpark security to tell Yosh that a friend of Judge Prentice Marshall was hoping to see him. Then, and only then, was she granted permission to gain access to the Cubs clubhouse.

In 1999, Harry Caray's second restaurant opened in Rosemont. Along with Yosh, we attended the grand opening. Randy Hundley, the former Cubs catcher was there. He had been filling in as a color commentator on Cubs radio broadcasts. His son, Todd, also a catcher, was having a terrific year with the Los Angeles Dodgers. In every broadcast, Randy would give an update on Todd's accomplishments. These updates were so frequent that it seemed Todd was a member of the Cubs. Upon seeing Randy, feigning ignorance, we asked him, "How is your son, Todd, doing?"

In 2000, the Cubs were on the road and late one afternoon we visited Yosh in the Cubs clubhouse. Anne was working nearby and came to pick up Tony for the drive home. Anne came to the clubhouse to meet Yosh and told him she had to use the restroom. Yosh instructed Anne to use the personal restroom of Don Baylor, the Cubs manager. Yosh told Anne to make sure she put the seat back up after she was done so Don would not know someone had used it!

Also in 2000, we had the honor of joining Yosh at the dinner honoring the Cubs 1900-1999 All-Century team. As Cubs fans since early childhood, this was a special treat.

We also had the opportunity to meet another child hero, Jim Hickman. He was one of Yosh's all-time favorite players. Fresh in our minds was an excited Jack Brickhouse announcing, "Hickman has hit another one! Way to go Hick! Hoo Wee!"

In 2001, Yosh became assistant visiting clubhouse manger under Dana Noeltner after approximately 50 years as home clubhouse manager. We would often help Dana and Yosh unpack the visiting team's equipment would arrive late at night and assist in packing the equipment when the team left Wrigley. Yosh was responsible for doing the laundry after the game. We would wait two hours after games that we attended so that we could all go home together, particularly for night games.

On Saturday, June 22, 2002, Raymond Floyd, Jr. joined us for the game again against the St. Louis Cardinals. Before the game we visited Yosh in the Cardinal clubhouse and learned about the death of pitcher Darryl Kyle. The game was cancelled.

On October 24, 2002, then Giants manager, Dusty Baker's, 3 years old son Darren gained fame by running to home plate in the 7th inning of World series game #5 against the Angels. J. T. Snow saved Darren from harm, and from committing interference, by grabbing Darren and lifting him away when scoring. In 2003, Dusty became manager of the Cubs. The night of September 6, 2003 we drove with Yosh to Milwaukee for a night game against the Brewers. We had first row seats just to the right of the Cubs dugout. Darren and his mom were sitting behind us in the second row. For most of the game Darren sat on our laps so he could see his father in the dugout. The Cubs won 8-4. We all had a great time.

Through Yosh, we became friends with the Houston clubhouse manager, Dennis Liborio. Dennis got his start under Yosh's brother, Nobe who was the clubhouse manager for the Los

Angeles Dodgers from 1958 until 1991. At the end of July 2003, the Cubs had their family trip to Houston. In recognition of Yosh's many years of service, the Cubs gave him a trip to Houston. He had wanted to see the newly opened Minute Maid Park.

Nobe was also invited and the Cubs asked Carl to chaperone the Kawano brothers. They rode the Cubs plane to Houston for their weekend series against the Astros, July 25 through July 27. Tony was to go to Anne's family reunion in Kentucky and thus did not join. At the last minute, the trip was cancelled so Tony went by himself to Houston to join Carl and the Kawano brothers.

The games were held just after the Cubs had traded for Aramis Ramirez, Kenny Lofton, and Randall Simon who had joined the team. These players wanted extra early batting practice before the Friday night's game and the Cubs needed someone to shag the fly balls in the outfield. We borrowed players baseball gloves and roamed the outfield in Minute Maid Park under a dome! We had not had so much fun since playing ball at Sherlock School!

We spent most of our time in the Astros' clubhouse talking with Dennis. We were touched by the reverence shown Yosh and Nobe by Houston's biggest stars, Craig Biggio and Jeff Bagwell. Craig Biggio was playing centerfield for the Astros at that time. Minute Maid park was famous for Tal's Hill, a hill that rose in center field.

In the Saturday game Aramis Ramirez hit a long ball to center field that Biggio had difficulty catching resulting in a triple for Ramirez. On Sunday morning we arrived early to enjoy breakfast provided by the team. Biggio came in while we were eating and asked why we were there so early. We replied, "We want to teach you how to catch balls going up the hill". Later Craig graciously autographed a bat for us when he got his 3,000[th] hit.

While eating breakfast, the old school clubhouse managers, the Kawano brothers, bemoaned the introduction of food being served in the clubhouse. They did so as egg yolk and maple syrup ran down the sides of their mouths! We finished our breakfast alternating bites with laughter

Our game tickets were given to us by Houston. To quote Bob Uecker, "We must be in the front row." That we were, sitting in the manager's box. Cubs personnel were seating in the grand-stand. Some of the Cubs personnel were disturbed that we were spending so much time in the Houston clubhouse. After all, this was a Cubs family trip. We assured them that the players knew we were Cubs fans and that we diverted the player's attention by asking those in the on deck circle to go back into the clubhouse and get us a hot dog and chips!

Tony feigned kissing Yosh on the "Kiss Cam" shown on the video board!

Our friendship with Dennis paid greater dividends when he gave us the game day scorecard of the April 29, 2005 game that the Cubs played in Houston. Roger Clemens pitched against Greg Maddux. It was to be the next to last time two 300 game winners faced each other in a game. Dennis had the game scorecard signed by Clemens, Maddux, and Astros manager Phil Garner.

The last time two 300 game winning pitchers faced each other was July 19, 2006 when Maddux and Clemens pitched in Chicago. Tony told Roger that he loved his acting in the movie "Kingpin"! We have autographed scorecards of that game as well. Thank you, Dennis!

We are also fortunate to have the scorecard autographed by Greg Maddux when he struck out his 3000th batter July 26, 2005. Thank you, Yosh!

Dan Holian, the son of our good friend and client Lou Ho-lian, also served as Houston's bat boy. He was part of the famed Astro "Killer B's": Biggio, Bagwell, Bell, Berkman, and Bat Boy! Dan also served as Cubs bat boy for a game or two.

We have become close friends and golfing partners with Jim Hirsch. Jim served as Executive Director of our client, the "Old

Town School of Folk Music". Jim and his son Mike (now 30 years old) are Sox fans. Dennis agreed to have Mike serve as bat-boy for the Astros in a game against the Cubs.

When the Astros played the Sox in the 2005 World Series, Dennis set aside tickets for us. We gave two of the first game tickets to Jim and Mike. The other ticket we gave to another close friend, Robert Klaus, who was also a long time Sox fan. This was the game when Scot Podsednik hit the walk-off home run to win the game for the Sox We were in many ways returning a favor as through Jim, Tony had met Donovan, Joni Mitchell and Peter, Paul, and Mary.

We intended to go with Yosh to the second game. While standing outside of Sox Park before entering the game, Yosh confided to us that he had made a silent vow that he would not attend a World Series game unless the Cubs played. He told us that he did not go to the 1959 World Series when the Dodgers played the White Sox even though his brother Nobe was clubhouse manager for the Dodgers. We quickly gave our tickets away to a gentleman with two young boys who was desperately trying to secure tickets for the game.

Yosh also shared our newly found interest in golf.

Together with Tony's wife Anne, we all went to the final day of the 1999 PGA Championship held at the Medinah Country Club in Medinah, Illinois, a suburb northwest of Chicago. Tiger Woods, then 23 years of age, won his first PGA Championship. Yosh assured us that he would secure the necessary tickets. As of Sunday morning, we did not have tickets and began to worry. Yosh was "calm as a cucumber"!

He had left word with Tony Navarro, Greg Norman's caddy, that we needed four passes. Navarro told Yosh that the passes would be waiting for him at the concierge station at his hotel. Sure enough, the passes were waiting for us. Greg Norman had missed the cut. Included in the envelope were four passes, one of which was entitled "Mrs. Greg Norman"! Anne was thrilled.

Also, in the envelope was a "pink" parking pass. Upon entering the grounds of the Country Club, we were told that unless one had such a pass, parking was in remote lots. We flashed the pass to an unbelieving attendant.

We had our choice of parking in the "current participant" or "Former PGA Champions" section. Beholding Yosh's status, we parked in the latter section. When exiting the car, we passed by Bernard Langer. Yosh may have barely reached 5' tall, but he had friends in high places.

Later we joined Yosh in following Raymond Floyd playing in various Senior Tour (now Champions Tour) events. Raymond was a longtime friend of Yosh and a huge Cubs fan. Yosh maintained a locker for Raymond in the Cubs clubhouse.

One tournament, while waiting for Raymond to approach the tee box, Chi Chi Rodrigues came over to introduce himself. Shaking Tony's hand, Chi Chi asked him, "What's the most useless thing on a woman?" Tony replied, "I know you are going to say me, but I am going to say you". Among our childhood friends in Cicero, we learned to be quick in our responses.

In another tournament, Yosh and we followed Raymond around the course. Raymond was near the top of the leaderboard. Yosh was listening to the Cubs game on his ever- present headset radio. After most every shot, Raymond would come to the ropes and inquire as to the Cubs score. The Cubs were blowing another lead. Raymond proceeded to blow up in the tournament as well.

Ray also played a tournament at Harborside. When we arrived, we were told that the person to hold the sign following Ray's foursome giving each golfer's score in relation to par did not arrive. Exhibiting the multi- faceted skills of any valuable utility player, Tony became Sign Boy.

With respect to our golf, one day we walked and carried for 100 straight holes of golf at Glencoe's Public Course. We could have completed more before nightfall set in, but we had to wait for various foursomes to finish ahead of us. We were asked many times how we knew we could do it. We jokingly told those asking that the night before we finished 75 holes and that gave us confidence.

One summer a few greens were under repair. The flags were placed in the fairway near the greens. We all gave ourselves two puts on those holes. We noticed that our scores for the day were lower. By extension, using logic perhaps learned at Yale, we determined that the scores would continue to drop with more greens under repair. Continuing with that logic, we would accomplish our personal best scores if the entire course were closed!

One day, we took left work early to play golf at the Highland Park Country Club. The course was not busy, so they let us tee off as a twosome. Another twosome was ahead of us and after we finished our first hole they asked if we wanted to join them. We joined NBA Hall of Fame Member Scottie Pippen and then current Chicago Bull player, Nazr Mohammed. The picture taken could aptly be entitled. "the long and short of it!"

Scottie and Nazr also called us "Twin"!

Nazr Mohammed, Carl, Tony, Scottie Pippen

CUBS SPRING TRAINING EXPERIENCES

BEGINNING 1994 THROUGH 2006 WE would go to Mesa, Arizona to help Yosh pack the clubhouse for the trip back to Wrigley Field. We would pack the sports equipment, player personal items, and exercise equipment onto the truck. We would then meet the truck upon its return to Wrigley Field, unpack it, and organize the Cubs clubhouse. We would normally be in Mesa for the last two days of spring training and stay in Yosh's room at the Mezona Inn.

These are our fondest memories:

One time, we were able to take batting practice, batting between Mark Grace and Sammy Sosa. Utilizing the skills acquired in our youth at Sherlock School and in our alley, we did OK. There were no home runs over the "True Link Fence".

We batted against the pitching machine in the batting cage and played on the field with Dana Noeltner, Marco Herrera, and other clubhouse staff.

In 1996, we were walking to the original Hohokam Park from the Mezona Inn when a car pulled over. Luis Gonzales, then a Cubs outfielder, was kind enough to drive us the rest of the way.

Mark Grace was especially gracious. Mark has the major league record for most hits of any player in the decade of the

1990s. He remains one of the most popular players in Cubs history. Each year, when we entered the clubhouse, he would proclaim, "The twins are here. It's time to go home boys." We would sing out Thin Lizzy's "The Boys Are Back in Town" to anyone within earshot!

Tony, Mark Grace, Carl

We were permitted to watch the games from the dugout. Managers Jim Riggleman, Don Baylor and Dusty Baker were very friendly.

Just as with our time with the Bears, we befriended some of the younger players and subtly lobbied for them to make the team. "Hey Jim, Kevin Foster is looking pretty good!" "Oh Don, Scott Downs might be a welcome lefthanded thrower!" " Dusty, we like the way Michael Wuertz is throwing in his relief appearances!"

Tony told Scott that if he could not throw 95 miles an hours, he would be better off throwing 75 miles an hour. To boost Corey Patterson's confidence, Tony showed him Barry Bonds' early statistics, which were average compared to later years. To each prospect we asked, "Can you hit?"

At the end of the 1997 season, we were with Yosh in the Cubs clubhouse. He asked us to each sign a piece of paper. We did not know why. Just before the beginning of spring training in 1998, famed announcer, Harry Caray died. Yosh called and told us he was coming to Chicago for Harry's funeral and that he had something for us.

We told him he could give us that something when we came out at the end of spring training. When we arrived at spring training headquarters, Yosh gave us the surprise. He had Louisville Slugger bats made with our individual signatures. The Ruzicka twins now had their own bats. Billy Williams, the sweet swinging Hall of Fame Cubs outfielder, was especially excited.

The Cubs were leading the last game of spring training and starters were removed so they could pack up and get ready to leave for the airport directly after the game. The Cubs were leading by many runs in the 9th inning until Kyle Farnsworth (then on the minor league roster) gave up runs and the game was tied. There was only one player who had not yet played, Jeff Blauser.

The Cubs needed a batter in the bottom of the 9th. Billy Williams was serving as manager now and told Tony to find Jeff Blauser in the clubhouse to come pinch hit and if Tony could not find Jeff, Tony should bring his bat. Tony regrets to this day that he found Jeff Blauser. He envisioned taking a mighty swing and hearing Jack Brickhouse yell, "Back she goes, get ready now, Hey! Hey!"

In 1998, the Arizona Diamondbacks played in the newly opened Bank One Ballpark (now Chase Field). The Cubs played their last spring training game against the Diamondbacks in the new facility. We were fortunate to also watch that game from the Cubs dugout. When Mark Grace was being interviewed in the dugout as part of the Cubs Chicago television broadcast, we were alongside and were visible in the background. Our friends back home could not believe it!

Sammy Sosa gave us the assignment of guarding his game bats when he went out to warm up before the game. In the late innings many of the players came back to the dugout in their dress clothes. Sammy Sosa sat directly next to Tony and was wearing black velvet shoes. Sammy proclaimed, "Look at me everybody. I should be in the Hall of Fame just because of how I dress!" Tony asked Sammy if he was going out in public with those shoes. Sammy got upset. Tony told him he was only joking.

Once Tony went on the bus to a road game while Carl stayed back in Mesa. The game bats are put in a circular duffle bag. Yosh's explicit instruction to Tony was to bring the bats into the dugout himself when unloading the equipment. "Don't leave them out of your sight", Yosh instructed. "Unpack them yourself."

The arriving bus was met by personnel who brought everything into the clubhouse and dugout. Packed on the truck was the bat bag. A few minutes later while attending to the players, Tony remembered his stupid indiscretion and scurried to the dugout. There were the bats, all out of the bag. Tony hurriedly put them back in the bag before Yosh noticed. As we often say, "We didn't go to Yale for nothing!"

Once Yosh gave us the responsibility of stacking hats for a road trip. While observing our mediocre performance, Yosh exclaimed, "Who the hell taught you how to stack hats? Never mind, I'll do it myself!"

Another time we rode on the Cubs bus to Phoenix for a game in Chase Field against the Diamondbacks. We were sitting with Yosh and Nobe telling them how as kids our friends and us could all field. Billy Williams was sitting in the row ahead of us and commented, "you know what Rogers Hornsby said. Shake a tree and a lot of fielders will fall out but not many hitters." Our reply was that if we could not catch, we were never coming up to hit.

Yosh and we were always the last people to leave the park. The first day afterwork we all took showers. There was no hot water. Yosh said it had been that way all spring training. This seemed strange because the washing machine was directly on the opposite side of the shower and had hot water. We connected with the city of Mesa man responsible for the spring training facilities and told him about the situation. He examined it and discovered that the hot water pipe leading to the shower was blocked and made the necessary repairs. The Cubs had hot water in the shower for the final day of spring training.

We were two of the very few people that Yosh allowed to put players numbers on the knob of their bats. Certain players had two kind of bats: one with the customary rounded end and another with the end of the bat scooped out like a cup. These bats were marked with a "c" below the player's number, indicating cup. Sammy Sosa often used this type of bat. During the corked bat controversy, sports writers and announcers incorrectly thought that the "c" meant cork. Sammy gave us an autographed bat. We have thought of getting it x-rayed. Would an x-ray show cork if it is in the bat? X-ray technicians please let us know.

We pitched in with other clubhouse duties: passing out laundry, hanging up uniforms, folding freshly dried towels (the corners had to square up exactly), separate items dropped to the floor, by uniform, under garments and towels. We were back! Our experience with the Bears did not go to waste!

One game, Tony was ball boy, while Carl watched from the stands behind home plate. Carl enjoyed seeing the quizzical look on nearby fans who realized that we looked alike. Billy Williams told Tony that being ball boy was an easy job. Tony replied, "I don't know Billy. Sometimes the umpire will signal for two balls, sometimes for three. You have to be prepared".

In spring training 1999, we went to Phoenix Municipal Stadium to help Yosh at a game played against the Giants. In the clubhouse we met singer Eddie Money, who had joined with

Cubs pitcher Kevin Tapani in a celebrity bat venture. The game was held on a very cold day in Scottsdale with light snow showers. We became heroes of the relief pitchers as we brought hot coffee to them in the bullpen. With every two cups, we had "b(r) ought them two tickets to paradise".

Later, as Village of Glencoe President, Tony quoted Eddie Money. He successfully convinced the Village Board of Trustees to have the Village collateralize a mortgage so that the Glencoe Library Club could repair its roof. The repairs were necessary to facilitate the move of the Writers Theater (a popular venue featuring prominent, thought provoking works) to the Library Club building. Tony was severely criticized by a member in the audience. Tony's reply was: "to quote Eddie Money, "worse things have been done by better men'".

Those lyrics were from Eddie Money's song "Walk on Water." Walk on water would have a different meaning when Tony was Village Trustee and/or President. Much of northwest residential Glencoe as well as the 16th and 17th holes of the Glencoe Golf Club had flooding issues. The Village was to issue bonds to mitigate the residential problem. As a runner, Tony often ran on the Skokie trail alongside the Skokie Lagoons just west of residential Glencoe. He realized that much of the trail was often under water and discovered that the lagoons and trail had never been cleaned. As a result, sediment had grown over the sewer openings. From 1995-1999, the Chicago Audubon Society and Forest Preserve District of Cook County began a restoration program. Tony met with the County Board and the County dedicated funds for sediment removal. The Village did not have to issue bonds as the County correctly took responsibility.

The Chicago Botanic Garden borders the Glencoe Golf Club to the west. The boundary is directly adjacent to the 6th, 16th, and 17th hole fairways. As a golfer, Tony would occasionally slice a ball to these boundaries. When finding his ball, he noted that the Botanic Garden land alongside the 16th and 17th fairways sloped toward the golf course and that discharge pipes came out of the Garden to the 16th hole. Tony showed this to Garden engineers who agreed to address this drainage issue. Other members of our foursome do not allow Tony to take an automatic par on that hole.

Also, in the spring training in 1999, Glen Allen Hill was walking around the clubhouse naked. Yosh was a bit upset and told us: "look at him strut around", as if it were a bad thing. We replied that if Yosh and we looked like that, we would all be strutting too. Glen Allen later hit a home run that landed on the roof of the building across the street on Waveland Ave. It is one of the longest homers ever hit at Wrigley Field.

Before the 2002 season we rode with the team to the final exhibition game in Tucson against the White Sox. Carlos Zambrano pitched and did not do well. We stood leaning against the dugout rail next to Gene Glynn, the third base coach. We commented that Carlos was slinging the ball from a low delivery point instead of pitching from over the top. Upon returning to Mesa, we packed the players lockers.

Inside Zambrano's locker we found his minor league baseball card. The card pictured Carlos using an over the top delivery. Carlos had already left the clubhouse, but Robert Machado, his catcher that day, was still in the clubhouse. We showed the picture to Robert, who immediately recognized the difference in his delivery. Throughout his great career, Carlos normally got in trouble when slinging from the side instead of pitching with power over the top.

The last items packed were the Cubs exercise equipment. The equipment was extremely heavy and difficult to load on the truck. To us, it did not make sense that there could not be equipment both at Wrigley and Mesa. As Village President of Glencoe, Tony connected with the owners of the Multiplex Athletic Clubs, Hazel Gidlitz Ring and her family. They were willing to provide new exercise equipment to both locations for free in return for public recognition and ongoing publicity. We were unsuccessful convincing Cubs management of this value. It seemed to be a practical solution.

YOSH IN LATER YEARS

Y OSH LATER MOVED IN WITH Carl in Highland Park, a north shore suburb of Chicago. This was a lot of fun as Yosh set out on a new journey. In later years it became an adventure, just as Yosh's trip to and from the ballpark.

Yosh would take the 5:27 AM Metra North Line train from the Braeside station in Highland Park, transfer to the CTA stop at Main Street in Evanston, and then change trains to the Addison stop. He then walked the short block to his beloved Wrigley Field, arriving around 7:00. He was in his 80's during this time. As many of the fellow riders were of the Jewish faith, we referred to Yosh as "Mort" Kawano.

Tara Brown (Yosh's niece), Qian Yi, Carl, Yosh,
Frank Shorter, Anne, Back *Mitch Garner, Tony*

On his way home, he often fell asleep and missed his stop. Eventually he would call us from stations farther north and we'd pick him up. The calls would usually come from an unrecognizable cell phone number. When we arrived at the station to pick him up, Yosh was often in the presence of an attractive woman whom he had asked to borrow her phone.

Carl, Yosh, Tony, Don Hudgens

Carl, Raymond Floyd, Yosh, Tony

Later Yosh acquired a cell phone. This did not change things too much as we often received calls from someone who found a phone and called the most recently dialed number, one of ours.

Yosh became a fixture at all Ruzicka Family gatherings. Although he was only one year younger than our mother, Yosh called her "Ma". His favorite meal was our Mom's chili. Yosh spoke of going to Croatian picnics with George Metkovich, a Cubs player in the early 1950's of Croatian descent. Perhaps our grandmother was at those picnics. This resulted in another nickname, as we called him Yosh "Kawanovich"! We could almost taste the "rack of lamb" featured at the picnic!

We drove Yosh everywhere. Utilizing our Yale and University of Chicago degrees to their fullest, we had reached life's high note. We were chauffeurs for a Cubs legend.

He always wanted to go to the post office on Irving and Southport, the Walgreens on Broadway and Belmont, and the Chase Bank downtown. We told Yosh that any Walgreens would fill his prescription and that he could transact business at any Chase bank location. We showed him that at the corner of Scott Ave. and Green Bay Rd. in Glencoe there was a Chase bank and that a few further steps north there was a Walgreens. Both Glencoe and Highland Park have post offices. As the saying goes "old habits die hard"!

A major reason that the Cubs asked Yosh to retire was that in his later years he suffered from incontinence. We bought adult diapers for Yosh, but he never quite understood that he could urinate into the diaper. Instead he would run to the bathroom, try to remove the diaper, and end up wetting his pants and surrounding area. To show Yosh how the diapers worked, we spent one evening wearing only diapers while watching a Cubs game. We would let Yosh know when we were relieving ourselves. Yosh did not get it. Neither did our wives!

In June 2001, the Minnesota Twins came to Wrigley Field to play the Cubs. At one game, Gary Gaetti sang "take Me out to the Ballgame" during the 7th inning stretch. Joining the Cubs late in the 1998 season, Gary was a key player in the Cubs race to the playoffs. He was a star player for the Minnesota Twins from 1981-1990. After singing, Gary yelled "this one is for the Twins." After the game, Yosh told us how great it was for Gaetti to mention us!

Carl, Yosh, Ryne Sandberg,

Tony at Cooperstown

After the season Yosh and we joined Ryne Sandberg for dinner a night that the Yankees and Diamondbacks were playing in the World series. We had a tremendous evening, exchanging stories. On our drive home, Yosh exclaimed that it was the first time that the normally quiet, soft spoken, introspective, Ryne Sandberg had really "opened up". We learned that Ryne's nickname for Yosh was "Jonesy". Upon being introduced to Yosh, Ryne's father mistook "Yoshi" for "Jonesy". Ryne also gave us a new nickname based on that given to Ralph Sampson and Akeem Olajuwan of the Houston Rocket basketball team, "The Twin Towers".

On November 3, 2001 we joined Yosh and Nobe for a trip to Vero Beach, Florida for the first (and only) annual Nobe Kawano Golf Tournament. Vero Beach had been the long-time spring training site of the Dodgers. Nobe, long-time clubhouse manager of the Dodgers, was being awarded at a golf outing and dinner.

We would often discuss our autograph collection with our running friend, Bob Christiansen. Every time he asked, "Do you guys have Koufax?". We hit paydirt as Sandy was there. He is a member of Baseball's Hall of Fame and generally considered the greatest lefthanded pitcher of all time. Also attending were Duke Snider (also in the Hall of Fame), Carl Erskine, Ron Perranoski, Danny Ozark, and Ralph Branca. Yes, the same Ralph Branca that gave up Bobby Thomson's home run heard 'round the world".

Some of these Dodgers are featured in Pulitzer Prize winner Doris Kearns Goodwin's tale entitled "Wait Till Next Year". The book details her growing up in love with her family and her beloved Brooklyn Dodgers. The players were also featured in Roger Kahn's book "the Boys of Summer".

Duke Snider was a childhood friend of Yosh. They grew up in the Boyle Heights area of Los Angeles.

A "not so true" story we tell is of their first meeting on the local ballfield. The new boy in the neighborhood, Edwin Snider hit balls over the fence for a homer with regularity. The gang was awestruck. They had never seen anything like it! They had to give him a nickname. "King" was already being used by "King" Kawano. Instead, the boys nicknamed him "Duke".

A true story is that Duke Snyder's, daughter, Dawna married the son of a Japanese couple living near Chicago, Mitch Amino. Yosh and the Amino family had been friends for years!

Umpire, Bruce Froemming also attended the golf outing. Bruce was the umpire that called a check swing on a Milt Pappas 3-2 pitch to Larry Stahl with two outs in the ninth inning of the game held September 2, 1972. The check swing call resulted in a walk, thus depriving Milt Pappas of pitching a perfect game no-hitter.

At dinner, Carl ordered prime rib. Sandy had ordered a sirloin steak and had already been served. When the waitress brought out Carl's prime rib, it was twice the size of Sandy's steak. Sandy stated that he had been out ordered.

Sandy Koufax was one of the most popular of the Dodgers. To reach Sandy, people had to go through Nobe Kawano. We told Sandy that people trying to reach Nobe had to go through him.

The Cubs made the playoffs in 2003. We jokingly suggested that we were going to start a class-action lawsuit on behalf of Cubs season ticket holders. We purchased the tickets with the implied understanding that there would be no baseball in October. As fans, we always felt free to fill our October calendars with other plans.

In June of 2005, we and Yosh went to New York to see the Cubs play the Yankees. Yosh secured tickets from Gene "Stick" Michaels, a former Cubs manager who was then the general manager of the Yankess. "We must be in the front row"! At dinner, David Hyde Pierce, star of the television series "Frasier" sat at the adjoining table.

The next month, we joined Yosh in Cooperstown for Ryne Sandberg's Hall of Fame induction ceremony. One of the highlights of this trip was Anne getting her picture taken with Bill Murray. As Village President of Glencoe, Tony chaired the downtown beautification task force which recommended the Cooperstown style lights which were installed. It seems only fitting that in 2019 Glencoe celebrated its 150th year anniversary and Tony was one of the inaugural Glencoe 150 Hall of Fame inductees.

In late spring of 2006, we hosted a party at Tony's house to celebrate Yosh's 85th birthday. Yosh's family came in from Los Angeles and Raymond Floyd made a special flight to Chicago to attend. Yosh's sister Sophie exclaimed to Raymond, "You look a lot like Ray Floyd!"

Other attendees included Billy and Shirley Williams and former Cubs pitcher, Jim Brosnan. Jim wrote one of the first baseball books from a player's perspective entitled "The Long Season." It was the forerunner of Jim Bouton's book "Ball Four" which remains a favorite of ours.

We told Yosh that we were inviting his old friends Ted Williams and Joe Dimaggio. Yosh replied that they were both dead. We countered with, "we are trying to keep the cost down."

Everyone donned white floppy fishing hats which Yosh had long since made famous. Tony's daughter, Annette, made a series of Yosh baseball cards "Yosh through the Years" for each party attendant. We wonder if these cards were traded on the front steps of Tony's home!

We all sang him a song to the tune of a favorite Cubs song, "Hey Hey, Holy Mackeral". Lyrics were changed from "the Cubs are on their way" to "Yosh Kawano for the Hall of Fame".

In 2007 and 2008 we made a concerted effort with Jane Forbes Clark, chairman, and Jeff Idelson, Vice President, of the National Baseball Hall of Fame to get Yosh inducted into Cooperstown as a recipient of the Buck O'Neil Lifetime Achievement Award. That award honors an individual whose extraordinary efforts to enhance baseball's positive impact on society has broadened the games appeal and whose character, integrity, and dignity are comparable to Buck O'Neil's. We cannot think of anyone more worthy of this honor.

Thus far Yosh's signature floppy hat is on display but not his person.

Annette, Yosh, Carrie

Tony, Anne, Yosh, Carrie, Annette at Yosh Kawano Day

Our taste in music had started to diverge. Tony listened to some hard rock, while Carl, in search of true love and having no idea how to achieve it, listened to Air Supply and Dionne Warwick. In 2006 when Carl met his wife Qian Yi, he learned that one of her favorite groups while in Hong Kong was Air Supply.

On their second date Carl took Qian Yi to a weekday day game at Wrigley Field. She expressed astonishment that 30,000 fans were not working. At a subsequent game, Carl got the autograph of Jet Li, famed Chinese actor, who had just thrown out a ceremonial first pitch. Carl jokingly told Qian Yi that he was careful not to hurt Jet Li when shaking hands.

On another date, Carl and Qian Yi attended a Madonna concert. As a duet they sang "Crazy For You". Despite the "Borderline", their romance blossomed. To quote Harry Caray, "It could be, it might be, it is, Holy Cow"!

Carl and his wife Qian Yi were married in their backyard in July 2007. Yosh attended along with family members and friends. After the ceremony, a party was held at Tony and Anne's house in Glencoe. Carl and Qian Yi then went back to Highland Park, spending their wedding night in their bedroom which adjoined that of the Cubs legend! We are not sure if this was a "Hey Hey", or an "Oh Brother" circumstance!

At their wedding reception held at a later date, Carl and Qian Yi were introduced as man and wife, entering the banquet hall to Madonna's "Celebration".

On June 26, 2008 Yosh was honored by the Cubs in a pregame ceremony. We had the honor of joining Yosh on the field. Yosh threw the honorary first pitch. We practiced the pitch for many days. The pitch was a wicked fast ball, complete with numerous bounces!

In 2008, The Cubs signed Kosuke Fukudome from Japanese Major League Baseball. Although of Japanese descent, Yosh was born in America and never learned to speak or understand Japanese. The Cubs hired an interpreter for Kosuke. Yosh called us to excitedly inform us that the interpreter spoke both Japanese and English!

In the winter of 2008-2009 we visited Yosh at his home in Los Angeles. During our brief stay at his home we searched his garage for memorabilia, most importantly a signed baseball card of Jimmy Foxx. While we were unsuccessful in our search for "Double X", we did find pictures and letters from Raymond Floyd's sons, Raymond, Jr., and Robert.

The upcoming April of 2009 would be the first April since 1943 that Yosh was not working (or in the Army). He had always dreamed about going to Augusta, Georgia for the Masters Tournament. Raymond graciously provided Tony and Yosh with 4-day gift passes for the event.

Carl stayed home as it was tax season. Tony and Yosh stayed in Greenville, South Carolina and drove each day to Augusta. In 1992, Ray and his wife, Maria's home was destroyed by fire that burned everything. Tony humbly gave the letters and pictures of Ray Jr. and Robert to Maria. She was ecstatic!

Yosh and Tony saw caddies Steve Williams and Tony Navarro. Both were acquaintances of Yosh. Steve had caddied for Raymond Floyd and was caddying for Tiger Woods. Tony Navarro had caddied for Greg Norman and was caddying for Adam Scott.

Yosh knew just about everybody! Our friendship with Yosh certainly improved our chances when playing the game "Six Degrees of Separation". For instance: Yosh to Joe Dimaggio to Marilyn Monroe; Yosh to Frank Sinatra, Yosh to Eli Sargus to President Kennedy, Yosh to the Spilatro brothers (the movie "Casino" was roughly based on the plight of these Chicago mobsters). The possibilities were endless!

The Cubs were for sale in 2008-2009. We fancied putting together a conglomerate to buy the team. Tony was to approach actor William Petersen, who had been affiliated with one of our nonprofit theatre clients; Carl was to make inquiries with longtime Cubs fan, Raymond Floyd; and, most importantly, Yosh was to solicit William Wrigley III to repurchase his old team. Everything was in place!

One afternoon Tony received a call with no caller ID and no message left. He returned the call and it was answered by Mr. Wrigley's secretary. This was it! Yosh had done it!

Unfortunately, Yosh was merely hoping that Tony was in the area so he could get a ride home. We bet he asked an attractive young lady to place the call. To quote the lyrics from one of Frankie Valli's songs, "So close, so close, and yet so far"!

The Cubs were sold to the Ricketts Family for $845 million!

We also went with Yosh for the unveiling of the statues of Ernie Banks outside of Wrigley Field on Clark Street and of Jack Brickhouse on Michigan Ave. near the WGN studios. The latter statue was unveiled on a dark and rainy day. As it was unveiled, we were struck with how much it resembled Lou Boudreau, not Jack. As we left, we passed Jerry Reinsdorf, owner of the Chicago Bulls and Chicago White Sox. We could overhear Jerry discussing the statue with his friends, "It looks more like Lou Boudreau"!

In the summer of 2010, we were invited with Yosh to Andre Dawson's Hall of Fame induction ceremony. Andre was one of Yosh's favorite players. Yosh was now living in the Keiro Nursing Home in Los Angeles. His nieces and nephew received special permission for Yosh to travel to Chicago. The three of us then proceeded to Cooperstown. Arrangements for the entire trip were quite interesting, sometimes frustrating, but well worth the effort.

Each year we made a concerted effort to visit Yosh at Keiro to celebrate his birthday. As the years passed, Yosh became less and less coherent, unable to speak, and without expression. Our friends asked why we made the trip as it was not sure that Yosh knew we visited. We responded with the fact that we knew we did.

When the Cubs won the World Series, we were not even sure that Yosh was aware they won. We purchased a World Series ring with Yosh engraved on it and presented it to him May 28, 2017.

Yosh with World Series ring

On February 20, 2018, Yosh was inducted into the Cactus League Hall of Fame. As Yosh was no longer able to leave Keiro, his nephew Frank (Nobe's son) called and asked if we could accept the award on behalf of Yosh. What an honor. The Hall of Fame luncheon was being organized by Tim Sheridan, the Cubs long-time spring training public address announcer. Tim asked us to provide a picture of Yosh so they could make his HOF plaque and if we could provide memorabilia for the soon to open Mesa Sports Museum. We were happy to do so.

Nancy Faust, retired organist for the White Sox, provided the entertainment. We helped her and her husband move her organ into the banquet hall. As we waited for guests to arrive, we sang along while Nancy played some of the Bee Gees hits. Nancy asked us what walk up song she should use for Bob Uecker. Of course, we recommended "Wild Thing" by the Troggs, a song made famous in the baseball movie "Major League". "Oops, just a little outside!"

We accepted the plaque and each gave a short speech. Carl provided Yosh's history with the Cubs, beginning when he stowed away on the boat going to Catalina, Island where the Cubs trained, and then told one of Yosh's favorite stories:

YOSH KAWANO
CACTUS LEAGUE HALL OF FAME

Yosh Cactus League HOF

When the Cubs first moved their spring training to Mesa, Arizona one gentleman always hung around the clubhouse. This annoyed Yosh, as he was a stickler that the clubhouse was for players and coaches only. "Get out of here", Yosh implored, "you don't belong here." Rather than leaving, the gentleman asked Yosh if he could be of any help. Relenting, Yosh gave him a broom to sweep the clubhouse floor. The gentleman's performance was less than stellar. Yosh uttered his often- used refrain, "Never mind, I'll do it myself".

One day the gentleman was leaving for home and offered Yosh a ride to the hotel, but they would have to stop at the bank and the gentleman's home first. Yosh accepted. While in line at the bank, a man went up to the gentleman and asked him about the progress of certain zoning changes. A few steps later another individual stated that he needed help getting his nephew into Arizona State University. When they went to the gentleman's home, Yosh saw that it was a mansion, complete with household help. Looking out the back of his house, Yosh saw a spance of land. Yosh asked one of the helpers, how much land the gentleman owned. "Look as far as you can see, then keep going", was the reply.

The gentleman was Dwight Patterson, one of Mesa's most prestigious businessmen, civic leaders, philanthropists, and sports advocates. He was credited with luring the Cubs to Mesa for spring training, which earned him the title of "The Father of Cactus League Baseball." He is a member of the Mesa Thunderbirds Hall of Fame.

Tony followed with further information regarding Yosh and recognized the other inductees Gaylord Perry, Frank Robinson, and Bob Uecker.

He told the crowd that in addition to starting early with the Cubs, Yosh also started chewing tobacco early in life. We would drive Yosh everywhere and always had to make sure there was a cup in the car or that the window was open for him to spit. We told of Yosh often spitting on Carl's couch. Carl was going to write a book, "Me and the Spitter" until he found out that Gaylord Perry had already written the book.

Tony acknowledged the Cleveland Indians for being the first American League team to hire an African American player, Larry Doby; the first major league team to hire an African American manager, Frank Robinson; and the first team to lose to the Cubs in a world series in 108 years!

He stated that Bob Uecker did not receive near the credit that he deserves. The Cubs had just signed Yu Darvish. Yu had "Tommy John surgery". Tommy John was the first pitcher having that particular type of surgery and it was named after him. In Yosh's 65 years with the Cubs he witnessed many poor hitters that underwent the "Bob Uecker" surgery for which Bob did not get credit, "having the bat surgically removed from his shoulder."

Carl, Ferguson Jenkins, Tony

We gave the Yosh HOF plaque to Hall of Fame pitcher, Fergie Jenkins, for display in his sports museum.

Yosh died on June 25, 2018 at the age of 97. It was a definite blessing. We had an endearing friendship that spanned 55 years! A journey in and of itself.

Grant DePorter, the President and Managing Partner of Harry Caray's Restaurants Group contacted us and graciously offered to host a Celebration of Life party at the primary Harry Caray's restaurant on Kinzie street in downtown Chicago. The Cubs management was gracious in helping to send invitations. The party was a huge success. One of Yosh's favorite players Ryne Sandberg gave a speech. Other former Cubs in attendance included Rich Nye, Randy Hundley, and Mick Kelleher as well as tens of prior and current Cubs front office, ticket office, grounds crew, stadium, and clubhouse employees.

The celebration was just that, as everyone had great stories to tell about their experiences with Yosh. Steve Stone could not attend but made a video for the occasion. We are grateful to Grant, Duchie Caray, and the restaurant personnel that made the event happen. Annette provided "Yosh Through the Years" baseball cards to all attendees.

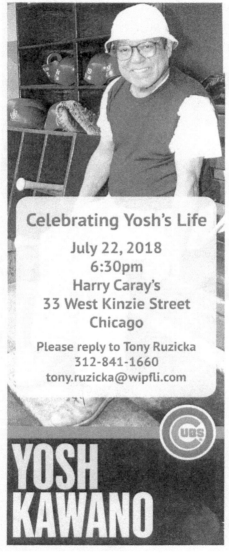

Celebrating Yosh's Life

July 22, 2018
6:30pm
Harry Caray's
33 West Kinzie Street
Chicago

Please reply to Tony Ruzicka
312-841-1660
tony.ruzicka@wipfli.com

YOSH KAWANO

Yosh Celebration Life

We take comfort that Yosh died with a Cubs World Series

ring. As we write this, we are remindful of Yosh's strict policy of the Cubs clubhouse being only for players, managers, coaches, and clubhouse personnel. We are touched that, somehow, we belonged! We suppose that being clubhouse boys for the Bears in high school has guaranteed us lifetime memberships.

As for additional Yosh stories, will we coin the phrase spoken by every true Cubs fan prior to 2016, "Wait until next year"!

Carl, Yosh, Tony last picture

CONTINUING THE CUBS JOURNEY

O
UR GOLF GAMES HAD NOT substantially improved. We were perplexed. We had the right equipment, we wore the proper attire, maybe we needed golf bags with our names on them! Or just maybe, we needed lessons. Through our many visits at the White Pines Golf Dome in Bensenville, banging golf balls with little purpose or technique, we formed a wonderful friendship with its proprietor, Mike Munro. PGA teaching professional, Chuck Lynch, taught at the dome.

We became and remain Chuck's students We have learned that just like in distance running, there is a science and methodology to improvement. Chuck, his wife Carrie and his family have become beloved friends. We have watched their son Matt and daughter Carly grow from toddlers to adulthood.

During the winter 2014-2015 golf lesson season, Chuck called and said he wanted us to meet a golf friend of his who had just moved to Chicago from California and that this friend was the father of a current Cubs pitcher. Chuck had told the friend about us and the Cubs. This friend is John Hendricks, father of Cubs pitcher, Kyle.

We were thrilled to make his acquaintance. We connected immediately. Kyle had completed his successful first season with the Cubs, winning 7 and losing 2 with an earned run average

ERA of 2.26. He graduated from a fellow Ivy League school, Dartmouth.

John's wife and Kyle's mother, Ann Marie, remained in California to administer her duties as manager of a Long Beach doctor's office. As we had our seats directly behind the Cubs dugout, John we would occasionally sit with us.

When Ann Marie would come to Chicago or when John's mother and sisters would visit, we would often let the Hendricks family sit in our seats. One game Kyle was not pitching very well, and his grandmother was perplexed. As a last resort, she had one last idea, "Maybe he will do better if I close my eyes!"

In return we would sit in the Cubs family section. We became acquaintances with many of the player's families, including Mike Bryant and John Rizzo. This proved beneficial for all.

When John sat with us when Kyle was pitching, we kept our distance. Whether it be Little League, Pony League, High School, College, Minors, or the Majors, John often would find a spot to sit near the left field foul pole to observe with as little stress as possible. He must be doing something right, because Kyle's home ERA is close to the best in Cubs history.

Often, we would pick up John at his then condominium in Evanston to take him to the game and then drive him home. Usually, we would wait for Kyle after the game in the Cubs player parking lot. While waiting for Kyle, we corralled various players and offered our advice. These players included Kyle, Starlin Castro and Javy Baez. Through their fathers, we made suggestions to Kris Bryant and Anthony Rizzo. If it worked years earlier for Clark Shaughnessy, George Halas, Larry Rakestraw and Ron Santo, maybe it would work again!

Starlin Castro's hitting prowess had been declining in recent years. The concept of "not overlooking the obvious" also came into play in 2015 when Carl asked Cubs hitting coach, John Mallee, to study Starlin's batting stance used in his 2010 and 2011 seasons, as opposed to comparing his current stance used in the previous year. Carl eventually pointed out the differences to Starlin himself.

Javy Baez famously bailed out while swinging. Tony said that he should imagine a beautiful woman standing right behind the pitcher. "When swinging, would you rather see the woman or us twins behind the dugout?". His friend agreed and reinforced Tony's suggestion.

At the time, Javy had just had some dental work done and was wearing a face shield attached to his helmet. We suggested he stay with it even after his dental work was fully healed. The shield would work like blinders on racehorses

Not bad for the "aliens" behind the Cubs dugout!

Theo Epstein facetiously said we should get a ring. We did not understand the facetious part.

Just as our uncles passed their love for the Cubs to our brother Tom, and he to us; so, too, has the love passed to the next generations. Tony's daughter Carrie and her wife Clara are special fans. Tony's grandchildren Brandynn, Keri and Uni have all attended Cubs games at a very early age. Brandynn and Keri are adopted children of Carrie and Clara. At one of their first Cubs games, Ferguson Jenkins gave each of them a personalized autographed baseball writing "Welcome to the Ruzicka-Just Cubs family". Our nephew Mike, Tom's son, is a terrific Cubs supporter. He, in turn, has passed this love to his daughter Martha. Martha is named after our Mom, her great grandmother.

In August of 2016, we all traveled to Colorado to watch the Cubs play the Rockies in a three-game series. Martha had fallen in love with Anthony Rizzo. We surprised her with Cubs apparel all featuring Rizzo! The Rockies video board periodically welcomed the "Ruzicka Velat Family Reunion". What a wonderful weekend!

Ruzicka Family at Cubs game in Colorado

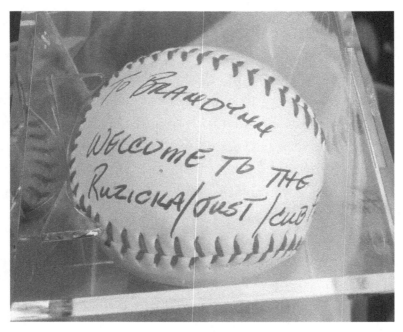

Ferguson Jenkins Baseball welcoming Brandynn to family

Kyle Hendricks finished 3rd in the 2016 Cy Young award vote for the best pitcher in major league baseball. He led the major leagues with a 2.16 earned run average. To honor Kyle, we made

CYle Hendrick t-shirts and a large CYLE sign (one letter held by each family member) for the World Series. The "CY" represented <u>C</u> y <u>Y</u>oung. We were kids again!

Kyle pitched one of the greatest games in Cubs history against the Dodgers to advance the Cubs to the World Series for the first time since 1945. The Cubs dominated the game. We counted down the outs. Unlike the famed "Bartman Game", our countdown did not take an ominous turn when we reached 5 outs to go!

Cubs Win! Cubs Win! We were going to the World Series! A picture of Carl celebrating the final out appeared on the back page of the "New York Post"! What excitement!

Once the Cubs won the second game at Cleveland, it was assured that the Cubs would play three games at Wrigley Field. Our brother Tom came in from Kansas to attend Game Four at Wrigley. Carl stayed home to watch the game on TV. During the singing of the National Anthem, the camera turned to the players, then to manager Joe Maddon, then to a full screen shot of Tom! Unbelievable! What a terrific reward for Tom being such a wonderful influence on our lives!

We appeared frequently on the TV broadcast as we cheered our beloved Cubs. We created the "It Is Happening" sign to replace the no longer pertinent sign, "Its Gonna Happen." We were beyond excited!

It is Happening sign

Carrie and Clara went to the last two games in Cleveland. We decided not to go. Superstition had set in! Maybe we will bring bad luck. We watched at our homes, resisting the urge to stand on our heads as we did when trying to break up Don Larsen's no-hitter in 1956.

All our family texted back and forth. Tom, Barbara, Mike, Matt, Carrie, Clara, Annette, and we texted with fingers busily and nervously punching our phones' keypads. When Cleveland tied the game in the eighth inning by Rajai Davis, our thoughts went back to Jack Brickhouse, "Oh Brother!" When the game went into extra innings, we could here Jack proclaim, "Any kind of a run will do it. Let's go boys!"

Cubs Win! Cubs Win! Cubs Win!

Hoo Wee!

Hey Hey!

Holy Cow!

It Has Happened Sign, Tony,
Carrie, Clara, Carl

The Cubs won their first World series in 108 years, breaking the longest championship draught in professional sports history!

On November 4, 2016 we joined Carrie and Clara at the Cubs' World Series Victory parade. The "It Is Happening" sign was changed to "It Has Happened"!

Who says, "There is no crying in baseball"?

Clara, Keri, Carrie, Brandynn

EPILOGUE

W E CHOSE TO, MORE OR less, end this part of our journey in 2016. The Cubs had won the World Series. We had waited 53 years for <u>our</u> next championship. This was 55 years less than the Cubs had waited for theirs.

In 2019 we moved our seats to the first row of what used to be the old grandstand. One game, while sitting with our good friend Ed Mular, we were greeted by various people as they walked past in the aisle just in front of us. Passersby included Doug Glanville, former Cubs and current sportscaster for ESPN and Sports Chicago; Carlos Zambrano, former excellent Cubs pitcher; Wayne Messmer, most famous for singing his stirring rendition of the "Star Spangled Banner" before Cubs games; and various beloved senior citizen ushers.

A gentleman in the row behind us jokingly asked, "Can I have your autograph?"

For our 70th birthday, we threw ourselves our own birthday party. We celebrated with approximately 150 family and friends. Our childhood friends, Larry Prochaska and Dale Bernard traveled from Dayton, Ohio and Indianapolis, Indiana, respectively. We had not seen them for about 50 years. Frank Shorter came in from Boulder, Colorado and our Yale classmate Shad Dabaghi traveled from Austin, Texas. Fellow runner Tom Boland came from West Palm Beach, Florida! What an honor! We danced to the music played by our guest performer, Ronnie Rice, of Chicago's own "New Colony Six", a rock group popular in our high school and college years. What wonderful lives!

Maybe it was time to write a book.

As we are writing this, it seems hard to believe. We can hardly believe it ourselves. Yet, using our beloved Grandma's favorite expression, "We tell you true!" Was our journey of pure chance? Was it one of divine intervention?

We realize that our journey started by an event that we had absolutely had nothing to do with. We were dealt a winning hand. Our mother had only had one-fourth of her ovaries, yet we were born to parents who gave us guidance, discipline, laughter and love. Our father died in 1996 at age 83. Our mother in 2010. She was just shy of celebrating her 90th birthday. Knowing that she was about to die, our Mom led us all in a chorus of "Roll Out the Barrel"! Both parents donated their body to science.

In freshman year English class, Tony had to write an essay on what William Faulkner was trying say in his novel "As I Lay Dying". Tony wrote that Faulkner was merely telling a story. There was no real purpose. On Friday, his paper was returned with a grade of "D". Over the weekend he happened to notice an article interviewing Faulkner in the "New York Time", a paper he rarely read other than the Sports section. When asked about what he was trying to convey in "As I Lay Dying", Faulkner was quoted as saying, "Nothing, I was just telling a story." Tony showed the article to the professor and his grade was changed to an "A".

Once while on Christmas break from college, Carl had excitedly planned to take his girlfriend to a Sunday night Blackhawks game. It was the hottest ticket in town. Carl was certain that he could somehow get tickets. If all else failed, Chico Maki would come through for him. Alas, such was not the case. He scrambled to find a source. As of 5:00, he did not have the tickets. He would have to "fess up" to his girlfriend that they would not be going. As he was prepared to make the call, our phone rang. A friend at Yale was offering him two tickets for the game.

Haven't we all had such moments?

Our lives have been like a fairy tale. Starting with seeing the picture of Bill Bishop, the stage was set for important life events that shaped our lives. One can draw a line from start to finish (as of today) that set -in- motion events that seem to be of pure happenstance:

1. Marilyn Bishop suggests we write George Halas to work for the Bears

2. Because we worked for the Bears, we ran track and cross country instead of playing football. We met Yosh Kawano of the Cubs and our Coach Don Hudgens.

3. Coach Don Hudgens, suggested we go to Yale

4. At Yale we met Frank Shorter and discovered that many New Trier High School students went to Yale

5. Tony raised his family in Glencoe, which is part of the New Trier School System

6. Through Tony's wife Anne, we began our career working together in accounting

7. Through Frank Shorter we became involved in running and the Chicago Marathon

8. Through our friendship with Yosh Kawano, we became intimately connected to the Chicago Cubs.

These seem unrelated, but they are all interconnected, causal steps. It is our lives' lesson and a lesson in family and friendships. We encourage everyone to cherish and embrace these relationships.

After our first encounters with our heroes, they became our friends, and these friendships mirrored those of our childhood playmates, high school teammates, and classmates at Yale.

No one ever knows what life has in store for us, but an adventurous, happy life can start out with a mere turn of the page.

We close by repeating our introduction. Hopefully, our journey serves as an inspiration to youngsters that many things are possible if an effort is made. Hopefully, it serves as an inspiration to professional athletes and to all adults that their interest in youth can truly make a positive impact.

Through it all, we have had the support and love of our mother Martha and father Tony, Sr; our sister Barbara; our brother Tom; Tony's wife Anne; their daughters Carrie and Annette; Carrie's wife Clara; Annette's partner Crawford; Carl's wife Qian Yi; Tony's grandchildren Brandynn, Keri and Uni; our brother-in-law; our sisters-in-laws; our nieces and nephews; and countless friends and mentors along the way.

Most of all, we had each other to share and shape our journey. Our thanks and love to all.

We hope you have had as much fun reading about our journey as we have had living it and writing about it. We intend to keep it going! Good luck to all of you on your respective journeys!

Get ready, George McCaskey, chairman of the Chicago Bears. Tony's 7 years old grandson Brandynn will be sending you a letter in about seven years!

As we are now 71 years of age, we are grateful to Baseball-Reference.com and ProFootball-Reference.com and Wikipedia, terrific resources we used to look up most of the game dates, player information and statistics sighted in this book.

POSTSCRIPT: FROM ANOTHER PERSPECTIVE

W E HAVE DETAILED OUR WONDERFUL journey from our collective perspectives. Many of the personalities mentioned are no longer with us. We have reached out to many of those still living to write a paragraph or so about their experiences with us twins. We humbly include these responses with great gratitude:

MARILYN BISHOP (WIDOW OF BILL BISHOP, CHICAGO BEARS DEFENSIVE TACKLE 1952-1960):

" O NE SUNNY MORNING IN CICERO, Illinois my husband Bill and I heard the doorbell ring. My husband and I answered and to our surprise there stood two young boys, eyes shining and with big smiles. They introduced themselves as Carl and Tony Ruzicka.

They lived in Cicero and knew that Bill was a player for the Chicago Bears. They were great Bears fans and wanted to meet him. There was an instant when Bill asked them to come in and talk.

Carl and Tony became fast friends. Bill thought it would be a great idea to ask Mr. Halas if they could become ball boys for the

Bears. When he approached Mr. Halas, he told them that they were twins, great Bears fans, and good workers.

Mr. Halas said they might be given a try, but the other teammates would have to approve of them and they would have to be good, steady workers.

Bill told the other players about the boys and they said they would give the twins a try. So, they came to the Bears dressing room with great smiles and full of energy. The players liked them immediately and approved them as Chicago Bears ball boys. Unfortunately, Bill had left the Bears and did not experience the twins' work first-hand.

This began and evolved as a great friendship. Bill always talked about how much he liked them and hoped his children would turn out like the twins. Fortunately, they did.

The twins have turned from being great boys to being great men."

NANCY MAKI (WIFE OF CHICO MAKI, CHICAGO BLACKHAWKS RIGHT WING 1961-1976):

" I REMEMBER THE RUZICKA TWINS WHEN they first came to our apartment. They were very appealing in their enthusiasm and, I must admit, in their physical sameness. If they'd been triplets, I would have had to adopt them. Their constancy was another factor in their continuing appeal over the twelve years with the Hawks, and it was to endure even past that time. There was a genuine luster to their love of sports, one that would not diminish as the years progressed.

It was fun to watch Tony and Carl grow up, seeing changes in them as the months went by in the summer and we returned to Chicago in the autumn. When I look back at it now, it was a privilege to see two lives evolving, especially of young men we believed in. Their enthusiasm never dimmed and so it was always energizing to have them visit us.

Talking to them now, when they're well into middle-age (or later) and have had successful careers as accountants, I believe, it doesn't surprise me that they have made the most of their lives. They did that when they were young, in their pursuit of and participation in professional sports. And now this book.... Well done, Tony and Carl!"

BOBBY HULL (CHICAGO BLACKHAWKS LEFT WING 1957-1972, HOCKEY HALL OF FAME 1983):

"I REMEMBER TONY AND CARL VISITING me in my glory days with the Blackhawks. They were special friends of Chico Maki, my linemate for many of my best years. Whether it was bouncing my son Brett on their laps or sharing their stories, the twins were enthusiastic supporters of me and the hockey team. In his later years, Chico would always refer to the twins as his true friends."

MIKE DITKA (CHICAGO BEARS TIGHT END 1961-1966, HEAD COACH 1982-1992, PRO FOOTBALL HALL OF FAME 1988)

"YOU GUYS WERE AND ARE the best. Great Bears Fans. You did a great job for us. Thanks for all your help, Da Coach"

JOHNNY MORRIS (CHICAGO BEARS FLANKER BACK 1958-1967):

"HOW COULD I FORGET CARL and Tony? They did every little job needed to keep us happy as players.

Remember, in the 1960s our Bears locker room at Wrigley Field was way too small for a 40-man football team. That is what made Carl and Tony's job even more difficult, "but fun". I am sure the twins would agree.

They did everything: organized our lockers, made sure we had all our equipment in place, cleaned our cleats, picked up towels, etc., etc. I could go on and on. Even during the actual game, they were busy and upbeat!

I like to think that their experience and success at their first job with <u>us Bears</u> helped them go on to Yale University and their successful business life.

Way to go Carl and Tony."

CLAUDIA TAYLOR (WIFE OF ROOSEVELT TAYLOR, CHICAGO BEARS FREE SAFETY 1961-1969, GRAMBLING STATE UNIVERSITY HALL OF FAME 1987):

"ROSEY HAD A SPECIAL RELATIONSHIP with the twins. I remember that they corresponded during the off season. Although Rosey was suffering from memory loss, spending time with Tony and Carl at the Bears 50- year reunion seemed to spark his memory. It was a special evening. I appreciate their care and friendship towards Rosey."

RONNIE BULL (CHICAGO BEARS RUNNING BACK 1962-1971):

"THEY WERE JUST A COUPLE of kids that were there to help. I remember them being twins that was relatively unusual. They were part of the group on Sundays!"

LARRY GLUECK (CHICAGO BEARS DEFENSIVE BACK 1963-1965):

" **A**S A COLLEGE FOOTBALL COACH for 28 years at five universities, I learned that the people behind the scenes in the program are just as important to the success of the team as the coaches and players. I speak of medical doctors, the training staff, the equipment manager, the field crew and yes, the clubhouse boys. They are all critical to a winning program. I was drafted by the Bears in 1963, the same year that Carl and Tony came on board as the clubhouse boys. We connected right away, and I watched as they took their responsibilities to heart. They loved their jobs, whether it was in the locker room, practice field and or game day. No task was beneath them and their willingness to be of service to the players and coaches was evident every day.

Congratulations, Carl and Tony, on your book. Coach Halas made a good decision when adding you to the Bear's family. You are part of the history of the Chicago Bears."

CHARLIE BROWN (CHICAGO BEARS DEFENSIVE BACK 1966-1967):

" **I** MET THE TWINS IN 1966. They were bright eyed, energetic, had manners, and were helpful at any turn. They appeared to always put their best foot forward. They conducted their accounting business with that same positive spirit. Always glad to see you. Always willing to lend a hand."

FRANK SHORTER (GOLD MEDAL WINNER 1972 OLYMPIC MARATHON, SILVER MEDAL WINNER 1976 OLYMPIC MARATHON, USA TRACK & FIELD HALL OF FAME 1984, RRCA

DISTANCE RUNNERS HALL OF FAME 1977, COLORADO RUNNING HALL OF FAME 2007):

❝I REALLY ENJOYED WHAT I WOULD call a "we just undercurrent throughout Tony and Carl's entire narrative. However, they did not "just" grow up in Cicero visualizing their sport heroes. They did not "just" wake up one morning and find themselves at Yale. Tony and Carl's social survival instinct that being twins could be an advantage was an early example of their always remembered street smarts.

As their childhood story evolved and their love of sports morphed into creative game playing, their innate intelligence had them always on the collective lookout for ways to reframe their way through and around all sorts of barriers, mental, physical and intellectual.

Developing sport skills led to simply wanting to always get better. Eventually, in what I would term a "Ruzicka Twins Direct Response" they tracked down their sport heroes, literally walking up to them to introduce themselves and then asked questions. Being twins got them in the door, but it was their combined talent that always seemed to allow them to stay there and never be shown out."

STEVE FLANAGAN (MEMBER U.S. WORLD CROSS COUNTRY TEAM, COLORADO RUNNING HALL OF FAME 2011, FATHER OF SHALANE FLANAGAN, AMERICAN DISTANCE RUNNER AND SILVER MEDALIST 2008 OLYMPIC 10,000 METERS):

❝TONY AND CARL RUZICKA HAVE written a well- defined and entertaining series of anecdotes about family, neighborhood, and Chicago professional sports. I only regret I missed growing up in Cicero within a few blocks of the Ruzicka twins! Play hard and laugh a lot!

My first exposure to this double shot of dynamic energy came in 1978, when I attended a sports trade show in Chicago. We were a new retail run specialty business trying to minimize expenses and they generously home-hosted our buying group from Colorado-based, Frank Shorter Sports.

Our post-show evenings with the twins were filled with many of the stories documented here. As baby boomers, the common theme for the Ruzickas and their listeners was a passion for ALL sports. Kids were often asked about their favorite sport. Most answered, "Whatever's in season!"

No surprise that Tony and Carl met and befriended so many Chicago sports celebs. Possessed with high sports IQ, and contagious enthusiasm, you can spend hours in depth talk on multiple subjects......and you'll walk away with a smile looking forward to seeing the Ruzicka again!"

HERB LINDSAY (U.S. DISTANCE RUNNER, SILVER MEDAL 1979 PAN AMERICAN GAMES 5,000 METERS RUN, WORLD RECORD HOLDER ONE HOUR RUN, RRCA DISTANCE RUNNERS HALL OF FAME 2002, COLORADO RUNNING HALL OF FAME 2010):

" **A**S A YOUNGSTER GROWING UP in Western Michigan not far from the Lake Michigan shore, I often looked out at the expansive waters and envisioned future connections with people and places across the big lake. Then, my only connection with Chicago was listening to the 50,000 watt AM radio stations, WGN and WCFL, and watching Lions vs. Bears games on TV Thanksgiving Day.

In my mid-20's my post collegiate running career was ramp-ing up and included travels to "the other side of the lake". Accountants and Yale alumni friends of Frank Shorter, Carl and Tony changed from business attire to running attire to host my first training runs along the Chicago lakeshore and introduced me to the local running community and races. As an elite runner of the day, I was impressed with the twins' fitness and race performances and was amazed they could achieve that while working full time jobs. Connecting with them over a span of years contributed to serendipitously making my childhood visions real.

Carl and Tony displayed their ability to create unusual and interesting adventures through their combined vision of possibilities. Meeting them, I was immediately impressed with their ability to get people talking and to connect them to their own adventures in sports and community. They were friendly hosts. Over the years, they transitioned repeatedly to new adventures with connections built on vision, curiosity, and unselfish sharing.

Years later, they gifted a ticket for me to experience the friendly confines of Wrigley Field from Tommy's row 1 seat behind the Cubs dugout. Wow! What connections they have created and shared. I am grateful for being part of their unusual adventures. I think you will enjoy reading about them and the connections that made them possible."

LEE FLAHERTY (FOUNDER CHICAGO MARATHON):

"MEASURED FOR HISTORY." THE INAUGURAL 1977 Mayor Daley Marathon was uniquely owned by taxpayers, encouraged female runners to participate, was the largest startup with 5214 runners, and had global media showcasing Chicago. Chicagoans were celebrating enthusiastically and, then, the joy was shattered.

New York Marathon directors claimed Chicago's course was short and the race would not be sanctioned worldwide. They arrived in Chicago with experienced experts using elaborate devices and measured Chicago's 26.2 mile course not once, but three times. With embarrassment, the amazed directors found the course was long by one yard. I was not surprised because Tony and Carl Ruzicka, seasoned runners, Yale grads, and dedicated volunteers, measured the course exactly. Then, as certified public accountants, knowing a startup marathon would be challenged, they added 36 inches to the course.

In 1978, The President's Council on Physical Fitness and Sports selected Chicago's Marathon the model for America and I accepted the honor for the Gold Medal volunteers who did the work. I told President Jimmy Carter: "We were fortunate that Tony and Carl Ruzicka, with precision and vision, measured the Chicago Marathon course as it will be part of history."

In 1980, at Tony and Carl's suggestion and direction, the marathon presented a first-ever charity pledge program. Over 43 years, the Chicago Marathon has achieved historical recognition! Thanks Tony and Carl."

BILLY WILLIAMS (CHICAGO CUBS OUTFIELDER, 1959-1974, CUBS COACH 1980-1982, 1986-1987, 1992-2001, NATIONAL BASEBALL HALL OF FAME 1987):

" I ALWAYS ENJOYED THE TIME SPENT with Tony and Carl when they came out at the end of spring training to help out Yosh Kawano. I shared their excitement when Yosh presented them with their very own bats. During the last few games, I always told them to be prepared to pinch hit. At Wrigley, to get my attention, the twins would always yell out my nickname, "Whistler". Upon seeing them sitting behind the dugout, I would always ask them if they brought their bats along, just in case. My wife Shirley and I enjoyed Yosh's 85th birthday celebration. Friends of Yosh are always friends of mine."

MARK GRACE (CHICAGO CUBS FIRST BASEMAN 1988-2000):

"Tony and Carl were, and still are, Chicago sports staples. I'll always remember our iconic clubhouse manager, Yosh Kawano, introducing them to me early in my career. I thought, "Hmm, these twins must be really good guys if Yosh allows them in the clubhouse." It didn't take long for me to realize just how correct I was.

Shortly thereafter, when I'd be sitting at my locker having my 9am coffee, Yosh would approach me and say, "Gracie, the twins are coming today!" He knew how much I enjoyed and appreciated those rascals.

I know Tony and Carl have a million stories to tell. I just hope they don't tell all the things they know about me! Ha!

But on a serious note, the twins were a major part of my 13 years in Cubs blue. They were always available to help me and/ or my teammates with anything and asked for nothing in return. Cheers, Tony and Carl!"

JIM RIGGLEMAN (CHICAGO CUBS MANAGER 1995-1999):

"Carl and Tony Ruzicka are twin brothers with great history both at Wrigley Field and inside the clubhouse. Many fans are deemed as loyal, but none could be more so than these two.

I first got to know them through coaches and Yosh Kawano, all of whom had been Cubs long before me. The twins had that wonderful ability to be both supportive to me, but not to be an overbearing presence. They always offered help on areas away from the ballpark, such as recommendations for housing, restaurants, transportation, etc.

Never was there a comment concerning the team as far as winning or losing. No matter if we struggled or won, the twins loved the Cubs and were totally supportive.

I loved Yosh. The fact that Carl and Tony were trusted and befriended by Yosh was verification that these two could be counted on.

A smile and a wave were generally the extent of our communication while I was with the Cubs. But it was nice to know that they would be there for you if needed.

As I came back to Chicago with other teams, the twins treated me as a friend and as if I had never left. We would meet down by the dugout and catch up every time I came in. They were always upbeat about the Cubs and gave me updates on Yosh's condition.

Carl and Tony are, and always have been, a big part of my great feelings about the Cubs and Wrigley Field."

RAYMOND FLOYD (WINNER GOLF'S MASTERS TOURNAMENT, PGA CHAMPIONSHIP, AND U.S. OPEN, WORLD GOLF HALL OF FAME 1989):

"IT IS ONLY FITTING THAT I met Tony and Carl when attending a Cubs game at Wrigley Field. Afterwards, along with Yosh Kawano, my great friend, we went out to dinner at Binyon's restaurant in Chicago's loop. The twins' affection for Yosh was obvious, as was Yosh's affection for the two of them.

I was privileged to know Yosh for many years. We became especially close during the Cubs glory years featuring Ernie Banks, Billy Williams, Ron Santo, Ferguson Jenkins, and other great ballplayers. Because of Yosh, I was able to work out with the team and remain honored that I had my own locker in the Cubs clubhouse. At one practice, I joined Sam Snead as the only individuals to hit a ball over the famed Wrigley Field scoreboard. Of course, it was a golf ball hit with a golf club.

Although Tony and Carl were new to the game of golf, we seldom discussed my golfing career. Instead, we enjoyed reliving memories of long since retired Cubs players. Tony and Carl's knowledge of Cubs history is really something.

The party that the twins held for Yosh's 85th birthday was an enjoyable event. Tony's wife, Anne really knows how to throw a party. I was able to reconnect with Billy Williams and his wife Shirley, Yosh's brother Nobe, and his sister Sophie.

I enjoyed having Yosh and the twins follow me at various Chicagoland golf tournaments. The twins treated Yosh as their father. In the later years of Yosh's life, their care kept him going. They made sure that I spoke with Yosh each year on his birthday and regularly kept me apprised of Yosh's condition. I appreciate Tony and Carl's friendship."

CURTIS GENTRY (CHICAGO BEARS DEFENSIVE BACK 1966-1968):

" I REALLY ENJOYED MY TIME WITH the Bears and having the twins in the clubhouse. They made me feel welcome and took an interest in my play and in me as a person. I know them to be caring individuals. This was evident many years later when they helped sponsor an event raising money for an organization committed to empowering people with disabilities. They even took turns dancing with a wheelchair bound young lady."

Carl, Tony, Tom Barbara 2019

Ruzicka family 2019

Tony, Frank Shorter, Carl

Tony, Larry Prochaska, Carl,
kneeling *Dale Bernard*

Carl, Tony, Ronnie Rice (New Colony Six rock group)

Anne, Qian Yi, Carl, Tony 70th Birthday

CPSIA information can be obtained
at www.ICGtesting.com
Printed in the USA
LVHW022054130222
710818LV00006B/87

9 781735 588001